The Truth About Saint Joseph

Maurice Meschler, S.J.

The Truth About Saint Joseph

Encountering the Most Hidden of Saints

Translated from the German by Andrew P. Ganss, S.J.

SOPHIA INSTITUTE PRESS

Manchester, New Hampshire

Imprimi potest: Samuel H. Horine, S.J., Praepositus Provinciae Missourianae
Nihil obstat: Joannes Rothensteiner, Censor Librorum
Imprimatur: Joannes J. Glennon, Archiepiscopus Sancti Ludovici
Sancti Ludovici, die 10 Decembris, 1931

Sophia Institute Press
Box 5284, Manchester, NH 03108
1-800-888-9344

www.SophiaInstitute.com

Sophia Institute Press® is a registered trademark of Sophia Institute.

Library of Congress Cataloging-in-Publication Data

Names: Meschler, Maurice, author. | Ganss, Andrew P., 1875-1930, translator.
Title: The truth about Saint Joseph : encountering the most hidden of saints / Maurice Meschler, S.J. ; translated from the German by Andrew P. Ganss, S.J.
Other titles: Hl. Joseph in dem Leben Christi und der Kirche. English
Description: Manchester, New Hampshire : Sophia Institute Press, 2017. | "The Truth About Saint Joseph was originally published in 1932 by Herder Book Company, St. Louis, under the title Saint Joseph: In the Life of Christ and of the Church. This 2017 edition by Sophia Institute Press includes minor editorial revisions." | Includes bibliographical references.
Identifiers: LCCN 2017020152 | ISBN 9781622824526 (pbk. : alk. paper)
Subjects: LCSH: Joseph, Saint.
Classification: LCC BS2458 .M413 2017 | DDC 232.9/32 — dc23 LC record available at https://lccn.loc.gov/2017020152

Contents

Preface vii

Part 1

Saint Joseph in the Life of Christ

1. Saint Joseph's Home, Family, and Personality 5

2. The Espousals of Joseph and Mary. 13

3. The Journey to Bethlehem 25

4. The Presentation of the Child Jesus. 33

5. The Magi's Visit to Bethlehem. 39

6. The Flight into Egypt and the Return. 45

7. The Disappearance of Our Savior for Three Days. . . . 53

8. The Life of Saint Joseph at Nazareth 59

9. The Death of Saint Joseph 67

Part 2

Saint Joseph in the Life of the Church

Introduction to Part 2 75

10. The Shadow of the Heavenly Father 77

11. The Saint of the Childhood of Jesus 83

12. The Husband of Mary 91

13. The Man According to God's Own Heart 99

14. The Model of the Hidden and Interior Life 105

15. The Model of the Active Life 111

16. The Patron of Families 117

17. The Patron of the Afflicted. 125

18. The Patron of a Happy Death 129

19. Joseph Is a "Growing Son" 133

20. A Saint for All 139

Preface

Saints are like men and landscapes. Some people and scenes reveal their beauty and greatness in their exterior. It takes but a glance at them to compel our admiration, wonder, and love. This is not the case with the more modest of nature's phenomena. They demand a closer consideration and study; only then do their worth, beauty, and glory dawn upon us. It may, in fact, happen that their peculiar greatness lies precisely in their unobtrusiveness and hiddenness. The same is true of the saints. For as star differs from star, so do the blessed differ in brightness and glory (see 1 Cor. 15:41). Those who appear most unpretending to us may in reality be very great, even greater than all others.

Among the latter we number Saint Joseph. Not without reason does one spiritual writer call him "the most hidden of the saints." This is indisputably true in view of his exceptional position, on the one hand, and of his extraordinary holiness combined with his retired manner of life, on the other. For it was at a much later date than the other saints that he took his rise in the firmament of the Church's devotion; and in spite of the ever-increasing public veneration shown him, he still remains among the number of the less diligently studied of the celestial inhabitants. Of a truth, his obscurity is in a certain sense his greatness.

Since his star began to rise in the Church of God, not a few of his learned and enthusiastic admirers, thanks to their keen insight and their tender and resourceful affection for him, have thought that they have discovered great things about the saint and have proclaimed them to the world. Such are: his sanctification in his mother's womb, the assumption of his body into Heaven, and a number of other remarkable favors. All this may be true. God certainly imparted to him whatever became his position and ineffably sublime office. Again, we do not deny this; neither do we need it for our purpose. We have a surer, a really "prophetic word" (2 Pet. 1:19): namely, Holy Scripture, which avails more than all the private revelations and pious opinions of men, be they ever so probable.

What Holy Scripture says concerning Saint Joseph must be inviolably true. It frequently expresses in a simple word something great and momentous. To fathom its content, however, we have to delve deeply. A mountain lake charms us not only by its mirrorlike surface, brightly reflecting the heavens, but also by its limpid waters, which allow the eye to penetrate to its marvelous undergrowth of plant life, out of which merely an occasional water lily finds its way upward and poises itself on its bosom. Similarly Holy Scripture: its truth and simplicity disclose glimpses of mysterious depths. We have but to unearth the lore of Saint Joseph, hidden in the Gospel, to bring it to light and to make use of it in his honor. More is not required to obtain a sublime and singularly lovable portrait of the saint.

Hence, this little book in honor of Saint Joseph is divided into two parts. The first part, following the guidance of the Gospel, tells of the life the saint led on earth in the most intimate companionship with Christ. It is the actual life of Saint Joseph and the basis of all that follows. This life, although sufficiently well known, is always beautiful, attractive, delightful, and edifying. The second part contains, as it were, the afterlife of Saint Joseph in the Church on behalf of her children. This afterlife consists in the faithful's veneration of the saint and in the salutary effects that the various aspects of his life and virtues have exercised on the lives of the faithful. Something of the naïve, pious style of an older period would seem eminently suitable in writing about one like Saint Joseph, the simple, retiring, and humble man of Nazareth.

May this little work increase the number of admirers of the dear foster father of Jesus, and may the good God grant it His grace to bring this about.

The Truth About Saint Joseph

Part 1

Saint Joseph in the
Life of Christ

Chapter 1

⁀

Saint Joseph's Home, Family, and Personality

Saint Joseph's home was in the Land of Promise, the Holy Land. The latter is divided lengthwise into halves by the River Jordan. Starting from the snowcapped elevation of Hermon in the north, and cradled between the Mediterranean Sea and the extensive Perean deserts, the Holy Land extends to the south in the shape of a charming peninsula of ever increasing variety and multiplicity of uplands and lowlands, of meadows and green valleys with their tributary ravines. Galilee, with its wonderful sea and its undulating, shadowy eminences, within whose keeping Nazareth lies sequestered, was the loveliest section of the land; Judea, on the other hand, because of its rocky soil and deep, yawning chasms, presents a more austere and sublime appearance. In its interior, however, on a high plateau, stood the venerable Temple, the ancient sanctuary of God's indwelling and revelation and the center of the religious and political life of the nation; while not far away, on a windswept hillside, was poor but regal Bethlehem.

Palestine was, in truth, a place of habitation such as God alone could give His Chosen People in the midst of the nations of old, worthy to be His own special abode and the nursery of the divine humanity. Its three most hallowed spots, Nazareth, Jerusalem, and Bethlehem, were the fitting scenes in which Saint Joseph's life played a prominent part.

In this beautiful and renowned country Saint Joseph was far from being an unfamiliar stranger as regards kindred and family. He was a descendant of Kings David and Solomon, whose reigns represent the zenith of greatness and glory attained by the people of Israel (Matt. 12:42), and from whose family the Redeemer, the hope of Israel and the salvation of the world, was to descend. It was the most glorious prerogative of the Jewish people and the special distinction of the family of David, to prepare for the coming of the God-Man (Rom. 9:5). That this signal honor was conferred on the Davidic line is historically established in the unimpeachable genealogies of our Lord traced by the evangelists Matthew and Luke: by Matthew in descending order from Abraham through the family of Solomon; by Luke in ascending order through the family of Nathan to David, Abraham, and Adam (Matt. 1:1–17; Luke 3:23–38).

This genealogy is of the highest import to Saint Joseph, to his position and office, to his greatness and title to veneration; it is, first and foremost, the accepted genealogy of our saint himself. By means of it, he is proved to be the son of David and is placed in the closest relationship to the promised Messiah and God-Man, if not as a real father, nevertheless as a legally recognized parent. Thus, too, as regards the family of David, is the prophecy fulfilled that from one of its roots the Messiah would come forth (Ps. 88:30; 1 Macc. 2:57); hence, also, it is proved that the Savior is truly the Son of David, and that the whole glory of this family culminates in Him through Joseph in a very particular manner. For Matthew calls Joseph's father Jacob (1:16); Luke, however, styles him Heli, a difference that can be explained only on the supposition that in view of the Law of the Levirate (whereby a man was bound to marry the widow of his brother who had died childless, and thus perpetuate the latter's family), Jacob was the natural father of Joseph, while Heli was his legal father.

Hence, just as was apparently the case with Zerubbabel, the two branches of the family of David merge into one in Saint Joseph, who in turn transfers the glory of both ancestral lines to his divine foster Son. This descent from royal ancestors is in itself of little consequence to the Savior when considered as God, but it is a temporal title to honor, not to be underrated, when we consider Him as the God-Man. And thus our Savior is sprung from an ancestry of nineteen kings, a distinction He owes to Saint Joseph.

Hence, when the angel first addresses Saint Joseph, he styles him the "son of David" (Matt. 1:20). It is a Messianic mission that the angel is exercising, and it signifies that the great promise made to the family of David is now fulfilled in and through Saint Joseph. When, then, in the course of time, the people enthusiastically proclaim the Savior the Son of David, and in reference to this title confidingly invoke Him in all their sorrows and misery; and when to prove to His enemies His claim as the Messiah, the Savior Himself appeals to this name and title of honor (Luke 20:41), it is ever a recognition of all that He really owed to Saint Joseph. Saint Luke traces the genealogy of our Lord back to Adam, to represent Christ—as spiritual writers not without reason maintain—as the blood relation, lord, and head of the whole human race, the "firstborn of creation" (see Col. 1:15). Is not Saint Joseph thus implicitly designated patriarch in his relationship to the Church and to the coming generations of men? The patriarch Jacob in a dream saw a golden ladder that reached from earth to Heaven, by which angels ascended and descended, and at the top of which stood God Himself (Gen. 28:12). It is not in figures merely but in the very flesh that God took His position at the topmost rung in the person of the God-Man; and this rung was none other than Saint Joseph, "the husband of Mary, of whom was born Jesus, who is called Christ" (Matt 1:16).

But someone may ask how much of all this glory of the family of David was left at the coming of our Lord? What was still to be seen of all that worldly pomp in the workshop of Joseph the carpenter? What could he offer to Christ the Lord other than the doubtful prestige of a great but now obscured ancestry, and an external environment that was the portion of the lowly in Israel? This poverty and humiliation truly fit into the surroundings of Saint Joseph's life and are, moreover, among the characteristic marks of the Messiah, to be received therefore by Him from the hand of His foster father. Life's poverty and abasement belonged to God's plan for the redemption of mankind and were embedded in the vocation of the God-Man. With the exile of the People of God to Babylon in the reign of King Jehoiakim, the scepter passed away from Judah and the royal diadem from the family of David (Jer. 22:24, 30). Zerubbabel, as administrator and leader of the people, led them back to their ancient habitation. But the tabernacle of David crumbled away more and more (Amos 9:11); in fact, commencing with Zerubbabel's sons, Abiud and Rhesa, the family register silently makes its descent to Joseph with a series of entirely unknown names.

Until the Promised One should come, another family, the Maccabees, ascended the throne of Israel (1 Macc. 14:41); and after its bloody extermination the half-Jew, half-barbarian, monstrous Idumean Herod seized the kingdom (38 B.C.). Before his furious jealousy and fierce cunning, the descendants of David took refuge in flight; they hid themselves throughout the land under cover of private life and eked out their obscure existence partly by tilling the soil, partly by plying trades in Galilee or Bethlehem. Not a trace was left of the wealth of the kings who so readily multiplied in David's regime, nor of the worldwide fame of Solomon.

Of Saint Joseph himself nothing is known save that he was a carpenter; but where, whether at Bethlehem or Nazareth, we are not told. Joseph had, then, nothing in the temporal line to offer our Savior but his calloused hands and a heart full of devotion and love, and instead of the splendid pomp of the world, poverty and obscurity.

This was precisely what the Redeemer wished. For this He had come from Heaven. For this reason, too, He had ordained that the family of David should by degrees be reduced to poverty and obscurity. As God He could use neither wealth nor honor nor any other natural assistance. As God-Man, however, as the founder of a religion of humility and poverty and as the Redeemer from sin, impoverishment and insignificance were His proper instruments. The prophets themselves had represented Him in vision as a tender plant plucked from the royal cedar and springing up out of the parched ground (Isa. 53:2). The temporal decline of the family, the penalty for the sins of its forebears and representatives (Ps. 89:31–34; Jer. 22:24), became the sign of the Savior's appearance, a means to the accomplishment of His designs as Redeemer, and a bond of fraternal union with a much larger family than that of all the crowned heads of the House of David, namely, the poor and needy humanity, laboring and battling for its daily bread. Thus Saint Joseph also had to come. Thus he was for the Lord the acceptable, useful man, the father chosen from among thousands.

Impoverished royalty, then, was the temporal heritage that Saint Joseph brought to the Redeemer. However, neither royal blood nor poverty can of themselves exalt one before God. Only virtue and holiness avail in His sight; and Saint Joseph was a man of virtue, of great virtue and extraordinary holiness. We can draw this conclusion from the very office and position to which God had chosen and called him from eternity. God's decrees and works are always replete with wisdom and perfect proportion.

The nearer a creature approaches to God, the more intimate a sharer it becomes in His holiness. Now Saint Joseph was the head of the Holy Family, the legal father of our Savior, the spouse of the Mother of God; and this position brought him into daily and most familiar relations with both of them. From all this we may rightly conclude that the soul of Saint Joseph was a veritable well of grace and sanctity.

No office was like to his; no holiness, excepting that of the Mother of God, was comparable to his. At least as regards the saints of the Old Law, he must have surpassed them all in holiness. He is the last link of the Old Law, immediately connecting with the person of the Redeemer. In Saint Joseph the holiness of all his ancestors, who in the designs of God were to cooperate in the accomplishment of the Incarnation, must have reached its culmination and perfection. Like Abraham, Joseph was a man of faith and obedience; like Jacob, a man of patience; like Joseph of Egypt, a man of purity; like David, a man according to God's own heart; like Solomon, a man of wisdom.

We may draw a similar inference as regards the New Testament. Here, too, his position is unique. This much is certain, that his first appearance in Holy Writ shows him to us in the words of the Gospel as a "just man" (Matt. 1:19), that is, in the opinion of the fathers and commentators on Scripture, as a holy, perfect man, the term "justice" signifying perfection and sanctity. Only to Mary was he second in virtue and holiness. Of course, in view of his providential position, there is a toning down of color in his holiness, which allows us only a conjecture of the magnitude and glory of his virtues. His treasures of virtue are, so to speak, those of the lonely wilderness, in which only the heart of God and the eye of the omniscient Son could take pleasure here below.

Such was Saint Joseph. A noble, distinguished personage according to family and blood, he can trace his lineage as far back as Adam. He is a glorious personage even in his poverty and humiliation, for these were endured for Christ's sake. He is a venerable personage, because of his unfathomable virtue and sanctity; a personage, finally, specially molded for Christ, as needed by Him in carrying out His thoughts and designs for the restoration and redemption of mankind.

Chapter 2

The Espousals of Joseph and Mary

We are not likely wrong in assuming that Saint Joseph, "the man of the right hand of God" (see Ps. 79:18), did not concern himself much or anxiously about thoughts and designs of the future. Above all, his will and his endeavors were directed to the fulfillment of God's law and his own duties, and it was with confidence that he looked to the guiding hand of Providence (see Ps. 118:166). This is the best preparation for a truly divine vocation. Nor did Providence fail to manifest itself at the proper time.

Saint Joseph betrothed himself to the Virgin Mary, and she became his spouse. We are unacquainted with the details of the espousals. Our only sources of information in this regard are some remarks of Holy Scripture, a few references of the holy Fathers, the speculations of theologians, and various beautiful but altogether unreliable legends. Scripture merely says that Joseph was "the husband of Mary, of whom was born Jesus, who is called Christ" (Matt. 1:16); that he was told by the angel to take unto himself Mary his wife (Matt. 1:20); that he was espoused to the Virgin Mary before the angel delivered his heavenly message to her (Luke 1:27). As regards other sources and data, we can establish with more or less certainty three points concerning the Blessed Virgin that may bring us closer to the details of the espousals.

In the first place, Mary, like Joseph, was of the family of David. This is firmly based on the whole of Tradition and Holy Scripture (Luke 1:32; Rom. 1:3; 2 Tim. 2:8). She belongs to no other family line than to one of the two mentioned by Saint Matthew and Saint Luke; so that these family registers, although, properly speaking, they point to Saint Joseph's ancestry, nevertheless bring us into close connection with Mary.

In the second place, Mary must have been the heiress of one branch of David's family. We find no mention of brothers of the Blessed Virgin; otherwise Saint Joseph would not have led her to Bethlehem; and yet, as heiress of David, she had to be enrolled. Finally, at His death, our Savior commended her to the care of His disciple Saint John, a sign that, at that time at least, she had no brothers.

Thirdly, Mary had firmly determined, or had vowed, either conditionally or unconditionally, to preserve her virginity intact during her whole life. This is the only possible meaning of Mary's answer to the angel's message that she was to become the mother of the Messiah (Luke 1:34). These words, however, were evidently spoken after she had been espoused to Joseph (Luke 1:27). For, according to the prophets, the conception and birth of the Messiah were to be virginal (Isa. 7:14). No other kind of birth would have been becoming to the Son of God.

How did Mary under circumstances such as these come to be the spouse of Saint Joseph? Some surmise that her relatives, and particularly the priests, who were responsible for the maintenance of the legal status of the old families and, above all, for their perpetuation, had obliged Mary as heiress to give her hand to a man of her own kinsfolk (Num. 36:8). Mary recognized in this the will of God, and so consented to the espousals. Others offer a solution by looking at the matter from a loftier point of view. And their opinion, it would seem, the Church herself has commended, since in the liturgical prayer of the feast of the Espousals of Saint Joseph with Mary, she speaks of the wonderful guidance of Divine Providence in the event. Viewed under this aspect, the espousals are to be considered in a special manner the work of Divine Providence, which in its wisdom and power, in order to further the sublime purpose of the Incarnation of the Son of God, has found ways and means to unite these two chosen souls by the bond of matrimony, although Joseph, like Mary, had resolved to spend his life in perpetual virginity. Hence, God enlightened them in a particular way regarding their mutual intentions, assuring them that their entrance into the married state would not interfere with the resolutions they had made; and He made known to them His will that they should contract the marriage so that by mutual agreement they might faithfully fulfill what they had promised to Him.

The espousals were, then, the result of a singular illumination and disposition of God. Many fathers and theologians subscribe to this opinion.[1] It is certainly the most dignified and sublime view of all, thoroughly in keeping with Divine Providence, which knows how to direct harmoniously apparently irreconcilable ways to a common goal, in this instance none other than the Incarnation

---

[1] *Hom. in nat. Dom.*, formerly attributed to Saint Gregory of Nyssa, Saint Epiphanius ("*Haer.*" 78, I, 3, no. 7), and all who base their views on the legend of which we shall speak later; also Albert the Great, Hugh of Saint Victor, Saint Bernardine of Siena. Cf. Suarez, *De Incarn.* II, disp. 6, sect. II; disp. 8, sect. I.

of the Son of God. As only God could preordain Mary to be a virgin mother, so also He alone could give her a virginal spouse. "The man was just; the woman was just; the Holy Spirit, who was pleased with the justice of both, gave them both the Son."[2] Virginity is justice in a more sublime sense because it is a matter of supererogation.

The espousals, therefore, actually took place. Where, however, whether at Jerusalem, where Mary's family is thought to have had a home, or at Nazareth, is not known. According to Jewish custom, after the espousals had been arranged by proxy, the bridegroom would present to the father of the bride, or to the bride's guardian in the presence of her family and kindred, a ring or jewel as a token of his purpose; or the bridal pair themselves would express in words their mutual agreement to seal the matrimonial contract. In such a way, Joseph and Mary may have entered upon their espousals. Mary is believed to have been fifteen years old at the time, lovable and beautiful in form, and thanks to her careful training in the Temple, singularly accomplished in mind; moreover, as faith teaches us, she was unsurpassed in her sublime and wonderful prerogatives, bestowed on no other of her sex — in fact, on no other merely human being.

Concerning Saint Joseph's age, nothing certain has been handed down to us. But God's works are wisely ordered in every respect and arranged according to the highest laws of fitness and propriety. Hence, Saint Joseph may well have been older than Mary, likely in the prime of life, but by no means an old man. Thus, in the earliest centuries art represents him as beardless.

---

[2] See Saint Augustine, "Why the Genealogy Is That of Joseph and Not That of Mary," in *Sermons for Christmas and Epiphany*, Ancient Christian Writers (New York: Paulist Press, 1952), 63.

So, too, for the reason just mentioned he was certainly of noble bearing and of striking qualities of mind and heart. He was to be in every respect the worthy head of the Holy Family and its abiding support and consolation in the contradictions that would befall it. This would be possible only on the supposition that he possessed manly strength and singular qualifications of soul. According to the charming legend of a very ancient book,[3] the priests, in accordance with a special revelation received from the Holy of Holies in the Temple at Jerusalem, are supposed to have ordained that, in a manner like the one in which Aaron had been chosen by God to be high priest, all the young men of the family of David were to place a branch or rod on the threshold of the Holy of Holies; and the one whose rod should become green and blossom, and upon which the Holy Spirit should visibly descend, was to be the spouse of the most Blessed Virgin. Saint Joseph alone, whether from a motive of humility or love of virginity, did not present his rod; and thus no decision was arrived at. When the priests had instituted an inquiry into the affair, God answered that the rod of a man of the family of David was still missing. Joseph therefore brought his rod, and lo! it blossomed. The Holy Spirit descended upon it, and Joseph became the happy spouse of Mary. It is for this reason that Saint Joseph is often depicted with a blossoming rod in his hand, while upon its crown, even in very early representations of art, rests the Holy Spirit.

What is true of this symbolic legend is the fact that the espousals had in view a higher, really sacerdotal purpose; that in this instance, too, the origin of the choice was God and the Holy Spirit; and finally, that only their love of virginity sealed the

[3] *De Ortu Virginis.*

union of these two hearts for life. Virginity, in the eyes of Mary, was the precious ring that Saint Joseph offered and deposited for the possession of her hand. It was virginity, then, that was celebrated in these espousals, and without virginity they would never have been entered upon. This is why in the domain of art a lily is represented blooming forth from the rod of Saint Joseph.

According to Jewish law and custom the matrimonial contract was essentially sealed with the espousals. The solemn reception of the bride, or the marriage ceremony proper, was merely the external recognition and solemn approbation of the accomplished betrothal. Meanwhile this last mentioned solemnization was to take place on a later occasion and not without a painful episode full of deep anguish of heart for Joseph and Mary. For it was after the espousals that the great, sublime, and holy mystery of the Incarnation was enacted, which had such a decided import not only for Mary but for Joseph as well. Joseph, however, had no intimation of the occurrence, and Mary gave him no enlightenment in its regard. After the conception of our Lord, Mary carried out the behest of the angel (Luke 1:36) to pay a visit to her cousin Elizabeth in Ain Karem, and according to its purport this visit was the first manifestation of the Incarnation and application of its graces.

Saint Joseph, apparently, was not present at this visit; otherwise he would undoubtedly have shared in the knowledge of the mystery. Mary returned to her house at Nazareth about three months later, and by degrees the signs of the wonderful fact of the Incarnation must have clearly manifested themselves. Joseph, who naturally visited the house of his betrothed frequently, could not escape noticing the manifestation. How unexpectedly and painfully must the intelligence have impressed itself upon him! According to all natural appearances, he found his trust and honor wounded and betrayed. In spite of this, however, he was so filled with esteem for his spouse, and so firmly convinced of her holiness and virginal integrity, that no serious doubt arose in his heart concerning her innocence. Thus, disconsolate and perplexed, he remained silent, and Mary, too, kept her peace. This silence on the part of the Mother of God may be explained only on the supposition of the indescribable delicacy of her purity, of her humility and her heroic confidence in God, to whom she left the entire issue. And as regards Saint Joseph, it was his genuinely royal nobility of soul, his tender consideration for Mary, and his unshaken conviction of her holiness that sealed his tongue. He had sooner assume the existence of a wonder in the occurrence than allow a single shadow of distrust to hover over Mary's integrity. Meanwhile he had to come to a decision and take a determined step.

He could have handed Mary over to the law, or in private, in the presence of several witnesses, have dissolved the engagement without any statement of the cause. In doing this, however, he would to a greater or lesser extent have injured the honor of the Blessed Virgin. His good heart could not have borne that. To him, the best way out of the difficulty appeared to be to depart from Mary secretly, in spite of the sorrow such a loss would cause him, and leave the whole matter to Divine Providence. And this, in fact, he decided to do. He would rather have the suspicion of unfaithfulness fall upon himself than have the least shadow attach to Mary's honor.

It is under these circumstances that Saint Joseph makes his first appearance in the sacred narrative. He comes before us like an angel, beyond the reach of the lower impulses of anger, jealousy, and revenge, which in the Orient only too readily burst into a raging flame. He is a man of perfect self-control, full of tact and heavenly wisdom, and especially of eminent fairness, who, in spite of the worst indications to the contrary, does not allow himself to pass an unfavorable judgment on his neighbor. Holy Scripture very fittingly refers to him as "a just man" (Matt. 1:19). It is evident to us what a good choice God had made. Saint Joseph was worthy to be the spouse of Mary, the legal father of Jesus, and the head of the Holy Family. This event portrays Saint Joseph as already on the most elevated plane of perfection and holiness.

However, God Himself now interposed. He does indeed try His dear ones; still, He does not forsake those who trust in Him but hearkens to them, lifts them up, glorifies them (see Ps. 90:15). God sent His angel to Saint Joseph in a prophetic dream, which brought him as much certainty as if there had been a visible manifestation. The message conveyed to him a threefold enlightenment. First, the angel quieted him concerning his spouse, who was irreproachable and holy—the mystery that had been accomplished in her was the work of God, the action of the Holy Spirit. Secondly, the angel informed him that the child given to Mary was no less a personage than the Messiah, the Son of God Himself, who would redeem His people from sin; and hence, Joseph as His father was to confer on Him the name of Jesus. Thirdly, the heavenly messenger directed him to hesitate no longer but to take Mary as his wife. Such was the message; and could there be a more consoling awakening and a more blissful expression of his sentiments to Mary than that which followed on this visit of the angel?

How changed all was, and that at a single stroke. How glorious and sublime a being Mary now is in Joseph's estimation, in her capacity not only as saint, but as mother of the Messiah, a virgin, whose Son Emmanuel had been foretold by the prophets;

and he is to be her husband, her partner, her spouse. On the other hand, under what an obligation Mary now is to Saint Joseph because of his noble and generous heart. Thus, the bitter trial bound these two hearts together even more closely. And this was precisely God's design: to make known to each of the two the virtue and sanctity of the other, and to unite their hearts in esteem and love. Matrimony was intended above all to be a union, a welding together of hearts and souls.

The nuptials could now be celebrated without delay. It was customary for the event to take place at nightfall. In festive array and with musical accompaniment, the bridegroom, escorted by his friends, the so-called children of the bridegroom, made his way to the home of his bride, where she with veiled head and in company of her bridesmaids met the party. All now joined the procession, bearing torches and small lamps, and proceeded to the house of the bridegroom. Arrived there, the bride was presented to the bridegroom, their heads were adorned with wreaths, the marriage contract was drawn up, and the nuptial blessing given. Thereupon followed the marriage festivities, music and dancing, often prolonged through several days. Such was the custom in Israel. And we may assume that Joseph and Mary celebrated their nuptials in this manner. There is, however, no record of the place where the celebration came to pass, whether in the quiet hill town of Nazareth or in Jerusalem. At all events, the pomp that accompanied it was not that of the royal espousals of Solomon to which the daughters of Jerusalem had been invited (Song of Sol. 3).

The complications that preceded Saint Joseph's nuptials have become the frequent subject of representation in art. The following features are significant. In order to portray in a vivid manner the embarrassment arising from Saint Joseph's doubt concerning the virginity of his spouse, the artist in his carvings on the choir stalls of Amiens represents the saint in the very act of carrying out his resolve to leave her house. His wallet and mantle are already in preparation at his feet. He himself, worn out from the excitement of his tormenting fear, is in a sitting position and asleep, while to one side (according to Luini of Milan) Mary is quietly plying her needle in undisturbed confidence in God's providence. According to another portrayal at Amiens, Saint Joseph, enlightened by the angel as to the misunderstanding, with hat in hand casts himself on his knees and begs Mary's forgiveness for having proposed to leave her secretly; she in turn graciously grants the pardon by presenting one hand, while the other calmly rests upon the Scripture text, which she has been reading and meditating upon. At Amiens again is found the representation of how Joseph on a former occasion took the blossoming rod from the hands of the priest and deposited it at the feet of Mary, fully conscious of his unworthiness to receive her as his spouse. Luini depicts Joachim, Mary's father, tenderly clasping Saint Joseph in his arms while acting as witness of the espousals. An ancient prayer book pictures Mary as having departed from the scene of the betrothal and attentively engaged in reading a book, while Joseph, who accompanies her, is rejoiced at the sublime inspirations vouchsafed his spouse from on high. Both Gaddi of Florence and Raphael in their concept of the nuptials emphasize the quiet and recollected earnestness of Joseph and the trustful and modest serenity of Mary.

These are all practical, delicate, and touchingly beautiful strokes and embellishments, almost too exquisite to be true. Both earlier and more recent masters universally select the Temple as the devotional and hallowed background of the scene, or actually place the ceremony within its consecrated precincts. It was in truth a marriage contracted "before the face of the Lord," especially by reason of the illustrious virtues and sentiments with which the celebration was solemnized. In this event, all was simplicity, modesty, and eminent sanctity as became their virtuous adornments of modesty, their purity, and their godlike purposes of soul. The heavens and the angels hymn their carols; the Holy Spirit Himself is the festival's bridal joy. It is a betrothal before God and the Temple because the purpose of this union was directed to God and the Temple, the latter being the symbol of consecration to the Lord, of the Kingdom of God, in fact, of the God-Man who was to come.

Thus it was that Saint Joseph obtained his beloved spouse, Mary. The nuptials were really the work of Divine Providence, which by their means effected far-reaching results in every direction. The union was, according to the conviction of the Church and the holy Fathers, a true and genuine marriage. Saint Joseph is of a truth the husband of Mary and the legal father of Jesus Christ. Our Savior belonged to him as a son. The genealogy of Saint Joseph is the genealogy of Jesus. The descent of our Lord from David is thus legally established and is verified through Joseph's marriage with Mary.

This nuptial contract was the last preparation for the visible entrance of Jesus into the world. The fallen tabernacle of David had been set up again. The Ruler of the House, the Heir according to all the prophecies, may enter now with honor. The mystery of the Divine Incarnation, which, according to the wise designs of God, was to remain unrevealed for the time, is kept hidden by an ordinary matrimonial union. Thus, it bestows on the whole married state a sacred dignity together with privileged graces.

As a result of these espousals and the accompanying circumstances, Mary obtained in Saint Joseph an unimpeachable and, beyond all question, a sublime witness of her virginity, a strong and loving support, a faithful adviser, a refuge and a consolation in her difficult vocation. Both the married state and the state of virginity have in Mary and Joseph beautiful examples and powerful protectors. Their mutual labors, cares, and tribulations henceforward received a meaning and an importance for the whole Kingdom of God and were accepted by them as a cooperating share in the life of the God-Man for the redemption of the world. Finally, what advantages accrued to Saint Joseph from this marriage? It brought him the unspeakable bliss of daily and most intimate communion with Mary and, later on, with Jesus; it assured on his behalf the reverence, obedience, love, and gratitude of the entire family, the head of which he now was. How fortunate a man was Saint Joseph! There was not a happier and more honored man in all Israel.

As for us, the espousals teach us that matrimony in itself is a holy state of life ordained by God, and that marriages properly entered upon are really made in Heaven and are productive of indescribable blessings for the world and the Church. The espousals furthermore teach us that Divine Providence works from end to end mightily and wisely (Wisd. 8:1) through all sorts of apparently insoluble perplexities and, hence, that we can do nothing better than cast ourselves confidently into its arms.

Chapter 3

⁀

The Journey to Bethlehem

The days of Mary's expectation were gradually nearing their fulfillment. Then there went forth throughout the land a decree of the Roman emperor Augustus that all the subjected kingdoms, which included the Jewish provinces, should be enrolled together with their inhabitants. The census was ordered by Sulpicius Cyrinus, the governor of the adjacent Roman province of Syria, and was carried out by Herod agreeably to the ancient custom according to tribes, houses, and families, each head of a family being obliged to repair to the place of its origin for the purpose of registration. This order was the cause of much excitement and irritation among the inhabitants. Joseph and Mary, however, submitted resignedly and patiently; for they knew that all things come from God, and that the Savior was to make His appearance in this world in Bethlehem (Mic. 5:2). And so Joseph set out for Bethlehem with Mary because she, too, as heiress had to be enrolled.

Thus, the descendants of the old Jewish families hastily traversed the various ways to their native cities, not, as may be supposed, without some show of the prestige becoming their rank and station. The season was winter; the month, December; and since at that time of the year in the Holy Land strong winds blow and heavy rains fall, it may become bitterly cold on the hills. Mary and Joseph journeyed along slowly and modestly, recollected and patient amid the untoward treatment of men and the inclemency of the weather. Mary, heavily veiled, rode on the beast of burden that Joseph guided with the utmost solicitude. The journey lasted about three and a half days, leading probably through the plain of Esdraelon and the green valleys of Samaria, and down from Jerusalem over the plateau of Rephaim, where of old Solomon, seated in his gilded chariot and escorted by a hundred servants, rode to the gardens of Ethan in a manner far different from that of the Holy Family. Opposite the border of the latter plateau was the small but royal city of Bethlehem, situated on an elevation of terraced gardens and vineyards and surrounded by verdant valleys where flocks of sheep and goats were wont to graze. The little town with its fortresslike dwellings covered the crest of the western ridge of the elevation, while the eastern ascent toward Jerusalem was uninhabited and contained the grotto at the very site where the cupola-crowned Church of the Nativity now stands.

It was probably at evening, just as the sun was setting, that Joseph and Mary made their uphill journey through the terraces and came to the public inn of the city. Those inns (khans) are closed spaces where travelers may procure protection, rest, and water; all other necessaries they themselves must supply. In the present instance, however, the hostelry had been completely occupied, for Bethlehem was crowded with strangers. Hence, Joseph and Mary were obliged to continue on their way, until, as is likely, after knocking at many a door and being refused admittance by the inmates, they found outside the town on the eastern hill of gray limestone a cavelike shelter that served as a stable. It was probably known to Joseph or had been pointed out to him by some sympathetic person. There they settled themselves as best they could for their night's rest. In the Orient it is not extraordinary to pass the night in a cave, or even to dwell there temporarily. But in the present case and under such circumstances, this manner of lodging moves our hearts to pity. Mary and Joseph belonged to the most illustrious families of Bethlehem; they were the holiest of the children of men, the parents of the Messiah, for whom Israel and the whole world existed; and now this Messiah was to be born far away from the great thoroughfares of the world, unknown, unacknowledged, in a strange, unimportant region, as though He were just an ordinary person. He seemed scarcely to belong to the world.

Meanwhile night stole on, and in its holy shadow the Light of the World visited this earth. We may well believe that Mary brought forth her firstborn and only Son in an ecstasy of yearning and love, and as our holy Faith teaches us, without pain or any discomfiture. She beheld Him as a poor little infant lying in the fold of her mantle. She adored Him, raised Him in her arms, and having wrapped Him in swaddling clothes, placed Him tenderly upon the soft hay of the manger, which extended along the wall. When she had performed her first duties as mother, she summoned Saint Joseph, who was resting close by. He approached and beheld for the first time the face of Him, to see whom had been the desire of all creation. He gazed at the child, and supernaturally enlightened, he recognized His supreme greatness and glory in both His human and divine natures. Together with Mary he cast himself upon his knees, and before commanding Him as father, he adored Him as his God with a faith and reverence and love of which only his saintly heart was capable. Indeed, we may say his soul melted away for love and joy and gratitude to God.

The Truth About Saint Joseph

All his sorrows were now forgotten in the contemplation and embrace of the divine Infant, to whom he was to be father on earth. How this child must even now have ravished his eye and captivated his heart! What a joy was his at this gift of God and of his beloved spouse, Mary, to whom this divine token bound him anew in admiration and love. Only one regret was his: the unworthy surroundings of God's first appearance on earth and his own inability to offer Him at the present moment anything but his love and his whole heart. The impoverishment and humiliation of the royal family of David had here reached their lowest ebb. This circumstance touched Joseph's noble heart keenly. At that moment he realized his entire duty toward this child and made a complete sacrifice of himself to fulfill the office entrusted to him. It was his duty to support Mary in her services to the Child Jesus. Later on another Joseph (of Arimathea) would assist her in wrapping the body of her Son in the burial shroud and laying it to rest in the tomb. The swaddling bands and the manger are forerunners of the winding sheet and the grave. The divine Child saw and understood the sentiments and affections of His foster father and blessed him with marvelous graces for the fulfillment of his high vocation. By his first glimpse and embrace of the divine Babe he was clothed with an exquisite purity and wonderful sanctity.

This holy and blissful night brought Mary and Joseph a second surprise and joy. Scarcely had they offered their first homage to the Savior when the footsteps and voices of men were heard, asking for admittance into the cave. They were the holy shepherds, who, at the invitation of the angel, had come to see the Child and adore Him. They related to Saint Joseph how, while they were keeping watch over their flocks, the angel of the Lord had appeared to them and announced the birth of the divine

Child. Saint Joseph listened to their story with surprise, yet with feelings of confidence and joy, and led them to the Child and His Mother. The shepherds beheld the fulfillment of all the angel had told them and, having adored the child, reverently greeted His Mother, Mary. Filled with joy and praising God for all they had seen and experienced, they returned to their flocks. They remained staunch friends of the Holy Family and announced everywhere they went the coming of the Savior.

This wonderful nocturnal visit was a source of intense joy to Saint Joseph because it was a recognition and an honoring of the divine Child and His Mother, and in his regard, a marvelous strengthening of faith, which had received its confirmation from so unexpected a circumstance. The shepherds had become an object of affection and reverence to him inasmuch as they were messengers of God upon whom a ray of the glory of His Son had rested, and who had been accounted worthy to be addressed by His holy angels and to hear their heavenly hymn of praise.

The joy, with all its accompanying sentiments, that this happy night had awakened in the heart of the saint, has at various times found expression in Christian art. The earliest Christian age, heir and lover of objectivity and classical repose, is satisfied simply to place Saint Joseph (with a staff in his hand) next to Mary or near the manger or, as depicted in the Church of Saint Celsus at Milan, even with his carpenter's adze, thus representing to the world his official position of protector and foster father of a God, poor and abandoned by the world. During the Middle Ages, to symbolize that the saint was not the natural father of the Christ Child, he is depicted as still engaged in meditation or the perusal of a book, and even as slumbering nearby, as is shown on the reliquary at Aix-la-Chapelle. Toward the end of the twelfth and thirteenth and particularly in the fourteenth and fifteenth centuries, the portrayal of the saint's active participation in the birth of our Lord awakens to energetic life. Joseph shows the newborn Babe to the shepherds, as is seen at Saint-Benoît-sur-Loire; again he is shown standing and resting on his staff near the manger, contemplating the divine child with a look of tender and quiet devotion. In fact, his gaze increases by degrees into an expression of heartfelt fatherly affection; with hands folded he kneels with Mary near the manger, adores the Child, and, deeply moved, takes Him into his arms. The art of the present day remains more or less faithful to this concept. It would seem that with the increase of knowledge and veneration of Saint Joseph, art, too, had gained in vividness and pious intimacy in its efforts to depict the sentiments of his heart.

After the birth of our Savior, Saint Joseph probably sought a more suitable home for the Holy Family in Bethlehem and took up his abode there. The eighth day after Jesus' birth brought a new honor and a mysterious lesson to the saint. The child was to be circumcised (Luke 2:21). Circumcision was a ritual law of the Old Covenant and signified the separation of Israel from all other nations, the incorporation of the circumcised into the Jewish religion, and the acceptance of its law with its promises of blessings or of curses. The child at the same time received his name and thereby obtained his full status in religious and civil society. The rite of circumcision might be performed by the father or by a priest, but to confer the name belonged by right to the father. Our Savior, although not obliged to do so, wished to submit to the law in order to give it His approval, to fulfill it, and to take upon Himself the penalties of our transgressions of the law. Such is the meaning of our Savior's blood, shed this day for the first time. These drops of blood were a pledge that on a future day He would shed all His blood on the Cross for the redemption of the world. With awe and emotion Saint Joseph and Mary contemplated this blood offering. Did they not see in these drops of blood the threatening dawn that foreboded storm and tempest in the life of their beloved Child?

Such, too, was the meaning of the holy name of Jesus, which signifies God and Savior. It expresses, therefore, not only the essence of the God-Man, His human and divine nature, but also His mission and its effects in our regard. The holy name was to be for us a pledge of our redemption, of the forgiveness of our sins, of the hearing of our petitions, in a word, the pledge and intermediary of all blessing, all strength and consolation in life and death. For our Savior it was to be the pledge of His future exaltation, so that at His name every knee in Heaven and on earth should bow (Phil. 2:10). What our Savior is to us, that He wishes to be through the invocation of His name in the spirit of faith and love. Saint Joseph, in his capacity and with his authority of father, bestowed this name on our Savior, as he had been directed by the angel to do (Matt. 1:21). It is, therefore, manifestly befitting and proper to cherish a grateful and loving remembrance of him who gave this name to our Lord and opened to us this fountainhead of salvation.

Chapter 4

⌒

The Presentation of the Child Jesus

About forty days had elapsed since the birth of our Savior at Bethlehem, and the time had now come when Jesus was to be presented to the Lord in the Temple, and the sacrifice was to be offered for the purification of the Mother. As an acknowledgment of God's sovereignty over the Chosen People, whether as the source of all blessing in childbirth or as the liberator of Israel from Egyptian bondage, God had not only set aside the Levites as His peculiar property in place of the entire people, but ordained, moreover, that every firstborn child should be presented to Him and redeemed with five shekels. The presentation had to be performed by the father thirty days after the birth, or, in the case of a male child, even later (Exod. 13:2; 34:19; Num. 18:15); the mother, however, was obliged to free herself from legal stain forty days after childbirth by offering a lamb or, in the case of the poor, two doves (Lev. 12:6, 8).

Saint Joseph, therefore, bade adieu to Bethlehem with sincere gratitude to the people who may have befriended him, but above all with thanksgiving to God for all the many joys occasioned by the birth, manifestation, and circumcision of the Child who had been given to him there. The road to Jerusalem led again over the plain of Rephaim, which at this time was resplendent in the adornments of spring. Here it was that on a former occasion Abraham journeyed to sacrifice his son Isaac on Mount Moria. From the elevated border that crowned the valley of Hinnom the Holy Family could view on the opposite side the great city of Jerusalem with its pinnacled walls, the glorious fortress of David, the mighty Temple, and the verdant Garden of Olives in the background. Saint Joseph with his family spent the night either in the city proper or in one of its little suburbs. On the following day, at the hour of the morning sacrifice, he went up to the Temple with the Child and His Mother. For the first time the Savior saw with His mortal eyes the gorgeous Temple with its massive portals, bridges, enclosures, and the Court of the Gentiles, through which, by ascending the flights of stairs, the way led to the vast Gate of Nicanor.

There an old man, venerable in stature and appearance, seemed to be waiting for them. He approached them, bowed reverently, and stretched forth his arms toward the divine Child. It was Simeon. The Holy Spirit had enlightened and inspired him to come to the Temple to greet the Savior. Our Blessed Lady presented the Child to him. As one lost in rapture, according to Fra Angelico's unsurpassable representation, he contemplated the little one in his arms as one does a precious and familiar old portrait. At the sight of God's beauty ever ancient, ever youthfully new, his own heart, grown weary of life, became young again; and his lips hymned forth the wonderful song of praise that the Church even now recites every evening in thanksgiving for the blessings of each day of redemption. A marvelous, glorious vision, it seems, appeared to him in the eyes of the divine Child, in which he foresaw all the mysteries of the God-Man down to the vesper scene on Calvary. Above all he thanks God in his hymn of praise that his hour has come and that he has seen the salvation of the world. Now he is ready to die, for nothing really beautiful remains any longer in life to attract him. He then beholds the divine Light, which he raises in his trembling arms, as it sheds its effulgence not over Israel only but even the most distant isles of the Gentiles. But with pain and regret he sees this light as a judgment, and this child as a stumbling block and a sign that shall be contradicted for innumerable people throughout the ages, not only among the Gentiles but even in Israel. Deeply affected, he returns the child to His Mother and prophesies to her, her own fateful destiny under the image of a cruel sword that would pierce her heart and soul.

Meanwhile Anna made her appearance, a woman venerable in age, the living exemplar of the Temple, in which she had dwelt amid prayer and fasting from her youth. She, too, recognized the Savior and exalted Him as the Messiah, and her pale, careworn cheeks and dull eyes quickened again with youthful joy and happiness. To all who cared to listen she made known the momentous revelation concerning the Messiah.

Mary and Joseph were astounded at the ever-recurring and increasingly important and wonderful manifestation of their Child through such varied witnesses, both earthly and heavenly, and at the constantly growing prominence with which the vicissitudes of the child's life came into relief. This manifestation was, moreover, brilliant and glorious, being enacted in the Temple in the company of personages of recognized sanctity and in the presence of the assembled worshippers. Then, too, there were the important prophecies spoken concerning the Child. But Simeon, the just one, had inflicted a keen wound upon Mary, and upon Joseph also, in foretelling the child's future, a wound that knew no healing in the lifetime of either. "What will become of this beloved Child?" Saint Joseph may frequently have asked himself as he clasped the Son of his heart in his arms, and by degrees saw Him develop into the most lovable of the children of men, comparable only to the angels.

Joseph and Mary now passed through the stone parapet that separated the Court of the Gentiles from the Temple proper and ascended the steps leading to the bronze Nicanor Gate, glittering with overlaid gold. In this gateway, to the right, were two smaller entrances through which the women after childbirth and the lepers passed for the ceremony of legal purification. The women had to present themselves to the priest, and after a prayer and a blessing they were admitted to the Women's Court. Here were the large collection boxes with trumpet-shaped openings into which the money for the various sacrifices was deposited. According to the amount given, the private sacrifices of lambs or doves were offered after the morning sacrifice. Mary submitted to this ceremony in conformity to the example of her Son, who Himself had obeyed the ritual law of circumcision and presentation in the Temple, although neither she nor He was bound according to the intent of the lawgiver. Since the thirteenth century, art has represented Saint Joseph as a participant in this ceremony in that he carries a basket or cage containing the doves for Mary's sacrifice.

It was either after or during this ceremony that, through the father, the presentation and redemption of the firstborn took place. The part of the Temple set aside for this rite was to the left of the Nicanor Gate and at the middle southern entrance of the Priests' Court. There Saint Joseph, as the father, placed the Child in the arms of a priest, who, raising Him aloft and holding Him toward the Holy of Holies, offered Him to the Lord, and after the payment of the five shekels returned Him to His father while pronouncing the words of benediction.

Our Savior submitted to this ceremony, though needing neither consecration nor sanctification. The union of His humanity with the Second Person of the Godhead had sanctified and united Him to God in such a manner as no sacrament or ceremony could do. Never before during the time of the Old Testament had such a glorious sacrifice been offered in the Temple. Its majestic grandeur shed its radiance over the sacred edifice and throughout all the earth and all times, and caused the utter poverty and inadequacy of the ancient worship to be revealed in a more brilliant light. Now indeed did the new Temple shine with that transcendent glory that the prophet foresaw would come to it from the Messiah's presence and manifestation within its precincts (Hag. 2:10). All the sacrifices of the Old Law combined their brilliance in the splendor of this sacrifice; by it the ancient priesthood reached the pinnacle of honor and distinction, while God Himself stooped to earth in a more loving and condescending manner than at the dedication of the first Temple by Solomon. Here on Mount Moria it was that Abraham offered his firstborn son.

Another Abraham is here now offering his Son, but one incomparably more just and more pleasing to God than the first Abraham. It is Saint Joseph. Hence, he has been chosen by God to be patriarch of the New Law. And if Mary and Simeon and Anna were present with Saint Joseph at this ceremony and together praised God with the words "God is good and His mercy endureth forever; we have received His mercy in the midst of His Temple" (Ps. 117:1; 47:10), this would have been the first Candlemas procession, and it was formed by the most venerable and holy personages in all the history of the Church.

Chapter 5

⌒

The Magi's Visit to Bethlehem

After the presentation of Jesus in the Temple, Saint Joseph returned with Mary and the divine Child to Nazareth (Luke 2:39). Most probably, however, the Holy Family journeyed to Bethlehem again with the intention of abiding there permanently. For was not Bethlehem really the birthplace and home of Jesus? It lay, moreover, near Jerusalem, a condition that was an advantage to the Holy Family in many ways. Later on, too, when they had returned from Egypt, Saint Joseph again had in mind to settle down in Bethlehem.

The Holy Family had probably spent about a year in Bethlehem when quite unexpectedly there arrived at Jerusalem strangers, Wise Men from the Orient. With their blunt question as to where the newborn King of the Jews was to be found—for they had seen His star in the East and had come to adore Him—they threw Herod and the whole city with him into a fit of excitement and terror. Herod, the aged, bloodthirsty tyrant in the fortress of David, found no better expedient in his perplexity and crafty dissimulation than to inquire of the Sanhedrin concerning the birthplace of the Messiah. He communicated the answer to the

Wise Men, that Bethlehem was the objective point of their quest, and bade them go thither in search of the Child; when they had found Him, they were to let him know so that he, too, might go to adore Him. Thus the Magi reached Bethlehem under the guidance of the star, which to their heartfelt joy had again appeared to them on their departure from Jerusalem.

The country from which the Wise Men came was situated to the east of Judea. They were noblemen, Magi, perchance tribal rulers in possession of the sacred books. It had been intimated to them from on high that, when a certain extraordinary luminary made its appearance in the firmament, they were to proceed from their homes to offer their respects to the newborn King and Messiah. The star did, in fact, appear at the time of the Savior's birth or later, and they regarded it as their life's chief endeavor to follow the Heaven-sent guide. This much, at least, the star's appearance over the manger of the Savior leads us to infer regarding their innermost purposes. Thus, they arrived at Bethlehem and found the Child's abode pointed out to them by the star as though by a finger of fire.

Together with their servants and beasts of burden they likely took quarters at the khan of the town, and then sent to the Holy Family to inquire if they might be allowed to visit them, for they had come under the guidance of a star to adore the Child. Saint Joseph received the servants in his own gracious manner. And now the kings themselves appeared with their attendants, the latter bearing precious gifts that they had taken from the chests and saddlebags; for in the Orient, custom has it that no one shall come into the presence of a prince empty-handed. Our Blessed Lady, who had in her simple and accommodating way prepared for their reception, held the divine Child in her lap. At the sight of the holy Infant the kings prostrated themselves in a circle before Him; and with profound faith, reverence, and humility, with their hearts' innermost love and joy, they adored Him and offered Him both themselves and all their subjects.

Possessed of a noble and discerning spirit and truly royal hearts, they were not disturbed at the unacquaintance with the Child prevalent in Jerusalem, or at the simplicity and poverty of the dwelling of the Child and His parents. They cared very little for outward show and followed only the dictates of their simple hearts and of their faith as God had taught them. Thus, in the same spirit they took the gifts that the attendants had arranged in precious caskets on the carpet, and presented them to the Child — gold, frankincense, and myrrh. Gifts pregnant with mystery they were, symbolizing their own hearts' disposition, their faith, love, and adoration, and typifying the Child's divinity, royalty, and office of Redeemer. The divine Infant Savior looked kindly upon the scene before Him, knew full well the meaning of the gifts, and returned all with an outpouring of graces for them and their subjects, and blessed them as the advance guard and firstfruits of the Gentiles. Quite likely the Magi then sat down and conversed with the Mother of God and Saint Joseph, who in admirable simplicity entertained them by relating to them the more intimate circumstances of our Savior's coming. This is the first occasion on which the Mother of God instructed the heathen world, and Saint Joseph shared in the instruction. The Magi became Christians and brought the true Faith into their own countries.

Thus did they depart from the Child and Mary and Joseph with expressions of intense gratitude and heartfelt contentment and joy. They did not, however, return to Jerusalem. During the night they received in a dream the divine command to avoid Jerusalem on their journey homeward, for Herod had determined upon the ruin of the child. And so, the very same night, they with their retinue directed their steps southward along the way that leads across the Jordan. What they had seen, learned, and experienced was worth all their trouble. They had fulfilled their life's work.

Mary and Joseph rejoiced exceedingly at this remarkable visit of the Wise Men. Saint Joseph took a keen delight and pleasure in these holy men whose dispositions so much resembled his. He rejoiced above all for Mary's and his beloved Child's sake. Great honor had been shown to them. The wisdom of the Orient had come to do homage to the divine wisdom of this speechless Child. How gloriously the kingship of this apparently helpless Babe revealed itself. Hardly is He born and He begins to rule; although poor, He acquires gold and riches and calls His servants and adorers from distant lands; Heaven and earth obey Him, and His advent strikes terror into the hearts of His enemies. This event is the Tabor of Christ's infancy. May not Saint Joseph have thrilled with ecstatic joy and said in the words of Saint Peter: "It is good to be here, here we shall build three tabernacles" (see Matt. 17:4)? Who, moreover, does not discern in this mystery of the Gentiles' vocation a reference to and a type of the call of Saint Joseph to be the patron of heathen missions?

The exalted position Saint Joseph occupied in this mystery, which itself is a presage of the future glorification of the Church of the Gentiles, is most exquisitely and successfully expressed in a thirteenth-century mosaic at Notre Dame in Paris, in which the saint is depicted in a separate compartment under a canopy, resting on his staff in an attitude of meditation and apparently in readiness to receive his own proper homage from the Wise Men. A later painter of intense feeling, Fra Angelico, portrays Saint Joseph actually engaged in familiar conversation with one of the kings and earnestly intent on instructing him in the Faith. In another painting by the same heavenly gifted artist, Joseph, delighted at its costliness, is shown opening one of the caskets containing a royal present that he may offer it to the divine Child as a token of the whole Gentile world, of which Saint Joseph is the patron.

Chapter 6

The Flight into Egypt and the Return

The time had not as yet come to erect permanent tabernacles of peace. That very night an angel appeared to Joseph in a dream and brought him, the head of the Holy Family, the following message: "Arise, and take the child and his mother, and fly into Egypt: and be there until I shall tell thee. For it will come to pass that Herod will seek the child to destroy him" (Matt. 2:13). Such was the message. Every word of it entailed sacrifice and hardship. How many journeys our saint had already made since our Savior became so closely associated with him! Indeed, it seemed that rest would never be his. Flight is always hard; doubly hard is flight with one's wife and child, and especially flight into Egypt, that far-off, repulsive, pagan country. And for what length of time? To shield His people from Pharaoh and Sennacherib, God employed angels and startling miracles; for His Son He has neither.

Now what does Holy Writ relate of Saint Joseph? Joseph arose and took the child and his mother by night and retired into Egypt. There is no word of excitement, fear, or murmuring. This is Joseph, the man of obedience and confidence, the man after God's own heart. Joseph quietly awakens Mary and the Child. One glance at the sleeping divine Child tells all. If God even as a child wills to be persecuted with deadly hate, and humbly retreats from one of His creatures; and if He desires to remain unscathed through Saint Joseph's protection, surely it is reason more than sufficient for Joseph to do all, to suffer and endure all. They arose immediately and prepared their meager traveling outfit. Saint Joseph carries one portion; the rest, including the waterskin and the bag for bread, he places upon the beast of burden. Thus, while all the inhabitants around them are peacefully asleep in their homes, the Holy Family leaves Bethlehem in the profound stillness of night and takes the road leading southward toward Hebron. Neither reluctance nor unseemly haste is noticeable, only watchful solicitude and trust in God.

Thus is the scene portrayed in a thirteenth-century relief at Notre Dame in Paris. Saint Joseph is leading the donkey while he glances back at Jesus and Mary seated on it. Thus is his loving watchfulness portrayed. Fra Angelico, on the other hand, represents him walking somewhat behind the animal laden with the scanty household furnishings, his glance, free and trustful, directed to the distance; he is intent only on going whithersoever God called. This is an expression of his unshakable confidence.

For six hours the road led over the hill country of Judea through dense forests of holly to Hebron, the burial place of Abraham, Isaac, and Jacob, which nestled in a fertile valley. The journey from Hebron to Bersheba and thence towards the Mediterranean to Geraris through extensive meadowlands, which once upon a time Abraham had crossed with his flocks, took five hours more, unless we suppose that the Holy Family chose a direct route from Hebron past Eleutheropolis to Gaza on the Mediterranean, which would have taken some ten hours. From Gaza the broad, sandy way extends along the sea coast. The sparse vegetation continues to vanish more and more, and at the so-called Brook of Egypt begins the dreary dismal nine-day journey to the Nile. The road leads through the Little Arabian Desert, where the bleak, bare sand dunes are only rarely relieved of their monotony by occasional dark-green clusters of palm trees that tower above the moist depressions. The journey took about 150 hours and could be made in 30 to 40 days. When the Israelites of old were on their way through the desert, God sent them miraculous food and drink; we read of no similar heavenly condescension vouchsafed the Holy Family in their flight. Undoubtedly they, too, had to endure fatigue, heat, and cold along the route and many an inconvenience in the dirty khans in which the travelers from time to time sought shelter. But they bore all with quiet and contentment. The Child's safety was at stake, but this trial eventually passed, just as do all temporal things, whether they be joys or sorrows. At the first tributary canal of the Nile, the land of Egypt, like an earthly paradise of beauty and fertility, suddenly loomed up before the traveler's gaze. It is the land of Goshen, which the Israelites once upon a time inhabited. It is believed, however, that the Holy Family proceeded as far as Heliopolis in the vicinity of the present city of Cairo.

Meanwhile the bloodthirsty ruler of David's fortress waited in vain for the return of the Wise Men. He found himself outwitted and in his rage resorted to a most frightful measure. He ordered all the male infants born in Bethlehem and its neighborhood within two years to be massacred. The country was paralyzed with terror and dismay.

The Truth About Saint Joseph

Then was fulfilled the prophecy: "Rachel weeping for her children and refusing to be comforted for them, because they are not" (Jer. 31:15). Hardly a year had elapsed since the Holy Family, on their way over the upland of Rephaim from Bethlehem to Jerusalem, had journeyed past the tomb of Rachel, where Jacob had buried her with sorrowing heart. Little did Mary and Joseph then dream that the fulfillment of this prophetical word would be so soon accomplished, and that the region lying now so peacefully before them would so soon re-echo with the wild cries and heartbreaking moans of little ones because of the dear Child whom Mary bore in her arms and Joseph guarded so carefully. Herod, however, did not reach the very one whom he sought of all the innocent victims. The child was already safe in the land of Egypt, thanks to Joseph's solicitude, in whose fatherly arms He rested as securely as in an impregnable fortress.

The life of exile in Egypt, as may be imagined, was one of toil and suffering, but of joy as well. A pious tradition has it that Saint Joseph took up his abode in Babylon, a suburb of the modern city of Cairo, perhaps in a dark, narrow street lined with high buildings; there at least, even at the present day, a house is venerated as that which sheltered the Holy Family. Their sojourn there was linked with poverty and hence entailed a life of hard labor. Of old in this very region Joseph of the Old Testament, the type of the saint, reigned supreme as the all-powerful governor, second only to Pharaoh in dignity and authority; and fed the Chosen People of God with provisions from the granaries of the realm, which he had erected and thrown open to the public. Our Savior, however, preferred to be poor; and so Joseph and Mary were also lovers of poverty, and—assuredly not without many an inconvenience among people speaking a foreign tongue—nourished by the labor of their hands Him on whose bounty every creature depends for existence and life. Joseph plied the carpenter's trade, while Mary spun and did needlework.

The sight of the shocking idolatry that they met at every step must certainly have been a source of pain and discomfiture to the Holy Family. The taciturn Egyptians, otherwise so intelligent and cultured, adored all kinds of objects, even crocodiles, onions, and cats. The country, moreover, if we except the fertile, luxuriant, and charming borders of the Nile, was as monotonous and stern as the desert, which here comes into view on all sides. This environment, therefore, was not nearly so pleasant and homelike as was friendly Galilee.

But joys there were, nevertheless. For the Israelites, strong in faith, Egypt was a holy land with its memories of Abraham, Jacob, and Joseph, of Moses and God's Chosen People, which here in the shadow of pyramids had attained to a high degree of power, prestige, and development. The Holy Family was aware of this and drew consolation and edification from it all. Just at that time, too, there were many Jewish families in Egypt, and they had a beautiful temple built by the high priest Onias IV. No doubt Mary and Joseph entered into friendly relations with these families.

A higher consolation for them, however, was their spirit of faith and resignation to God's will. Even in Egypt they found God and with that they were content. Indeed their finest and most numerous joys were those occasioned by the divine Child. If we suppose the stay in Egypt extended over a considerable period of time, it was here that our Savior wore His first little dress, attempted His first tiny steps, and—oh, the bliss!—first broke the silence and with tender trustfulness smilingly called Joseph "Father" and Mary "Mother"—all of which are indeed very touching and heartfelt family and domestic joys. It was now that

Egypt received the benediction foretold in its regard (Isa. 19:19; Deut. 23:7). Perhaps, too, the future wonderful blossoming of Christianity and of the charming rose garden of mysticism, which with the erection of monasteries and the founding of monastic orders filled the empty desert with life, may have been a belated blessing due to the Holy Family's stay in Egypt.

We cannot say with accuracy how long the Holy Family remained in Egypt. The surmises range between a few months and several years. It is certain that the exile came to an end with the death of Herod. Death, which he had inflicted on so many innocent victims, eventually struck him down also by means of a pestilential disease to which he succumbed at Jericho. His sons divided his kingdom among them. Archelaus, his eldest son, just as cruel, hard-hearted, and dissipated as his father, inherited Judea. And now the angel of the Lord again appeared to Joseph in a dream and bade him return to Israel, because all who sought the life of the child had died. Joseph received the message with a quiet and reverential joy. With thanksgiving to God and to all the neighbors who had shown kindness to them, he departed with his family from Egypt. Having emerged from the dismal streets and bazaars of the Egyptian city, they returned homeward along the seacoast the same way they had come. Their hearts thrilled with joy as eventually they greeted the distant line of hazy blue, the wavy contour of the southern hills and ridges of the Holy Land.

Saint Joseph had intended to take up his permanent abode at Bethlehem. But from the known character of Archelaus, he had his misgivings about choosing Bethlehem as a place to live. In this state of doubt an angel advised him to go to Nazareth. Thus, they journeyed on through Joppe and along the foot of Mount Carmel, across the plain of Esdraelon and settled down among the hills and mountains that peacefully stand guard around Nazareth. For, indeed, was it not written that the Messiah would be a Nazarene, that is, one set apart, a sprout, a flower? And so Nazareth became the pleasant home and garden spot of Christ's youth, and Joseph was the protector and guardian of this flower of paradise.

Chapter 7

The Disappearance of Our Savior for Three Days

After the storm of persecution and banishment, the hidden life of our Savior begins, a quiet, delightful period of peace and home-like joys for the family of Saint Joseph. Only once was this peace disturbed by a passing, though keen affliction, when our Lord had reached His twelfth year and had developed into an attractive, amiable boy.

It was the Paschal season. The signal fires, customary in the Holy Land, announcing the feast of the new moon of the month of Nisan, were already blazing upon the mountaintops. The roads and bridges were set in order, and the entire populace made their preparations for their pilgrimage to Jerusalem to celebrate the principal feast of the Old Covenant, the Pasch. In the towns and the villages, various groups of pilgrims were organized, while along all the roads leading to Jerusalem numerous parties, arranged according to sex, made their way; and the valleys resounded with the chant of the Pilgrim Psalms (Ps. 118–130).

Our Savior had now entered His twelfth year, and, as the saying went, had become a "son of the law," that is, one obliged to

53

keep the prescribed fasts and attend the three principal festivals at Jerusalem. Thus, on this occasion He accompanied the travelers as a youthful pilgrim subject to the law. Nature was now arrayed in its verdant spring garb, and great enthusiasm manifested itself on all sides, especially so, when, resembling an island, the Holy City emerged from the deep vales back of the ancient sanctuaries of Siloe and Bethel on Mount Scopus, and with its mighty towers, walls, palaces, and cupolas and its golden Temple, broke upon their view like a heavenly vision. The Paschal pilgrims found lodgings with friends and acquaintances as guests, or for a small pittance were accommodated during the festival days. Thus, too, the Holy Family. At eventide of the fourteenth day of Nisan, the Paschal lamb was eaten; on the fifteenth of Nisan, the great sacrificial ceremonies that all the men had to attend were performed in the Temple; and in the evening of the same day, in the presence of the people, the first sheaves of barley were cut and brought to the Temple to be offered to the Lord and burned on the following day. After this offering of the firstfruits, with which the harvest season opened, the pilgrims might begin their homeward journey.

And this is probably what Joseph and Mary did. They departed from Jerusalem with other inhabitants of Galilee and Nazareth and reached the first stopping place, likely Beroth; but our Savior was not with them. Thinking He was in the company of relatives and acquaintances, they were at first not concerned about Him. But painful was their discovery that, in spite of all their waiting, inquiries, and search among the arriving pilgrim groups, He was not to be found and no one had seen Him. Solicitude and anxiety thwarted all their rest that night. But a still more sorrowful day dawned for them as they straightway set out on their return to Jerusalem. They sought and searched for the child on all the highways and byways, among all their acquaintances, and along all the streets; but nowhere could they receive any information as to His whereabouts.

Great was their grief, and tormenting their uncertainty and fear in His regard. Very special, extraordinary, natural, and supernatural considerations, the past and the future, faith and love were here combined to render their affliction extremely profound and acute. What had become of Him? Where was He? Had the sword of Simeon begun to persecute Him and perhaps smitten Him? Who can fathom the bitterness of their grief and tears? They had indeed suffered in their flight into Egypt, but still the Child was then constantly with them. Yet even in all their sorrow and bereavement they remained conformed to God's will, patient, and humble. Perhaps it was their own unworthiness that had banished Him from them! Nevertheless they thanked God for the happiness and honor that had been vouchsafed them hitherto in having His company, and the very loss of their treasure urged them with unflagging diligence to go in search of Him until they found Him. They traversed every road, and on all sides anxiously scrutinized each passing group. How sadly the Paschal season drew to its close; and they had hoped to spend it so joyously! Thus a day and a night went by, and a part of another day, before they arrived at the Temple, wearied and exhausted after their ardent search.

By a special disposition of Providence our Savior had hidden Himself from His parents during their search for Him. This was easily accomplished under the circumstances, since the men and women worshipped apart in the Temple, and in the same manner came and returned on their pilgrimage. He probably spent the night on the Mount of Olives or in a public caravansary, and begged a morsel of bread as an alms. After the departure of His parents on the following day, He proceeded to the Temple and made His way to the platform or lecture hall, where local and visiting doctors of the law delivered their discourses, during which the audience was permitted to ask questions. Jesus took His place among the listeners there, and, because He likely repeated His visits and drew everybody's attention to Himself by His winning presence and His intelligent questions and answers, He became the center of attraction for all, even for the doctors. Thus, too, on the third day, we may suppose, He appeared in the lecture room, and on that occasion filled all with wonder and astonishment by His extraordinary wisdom and superior endowments. The doctors themselves rose from their seats of honor, and, placing themselves beside Him, questioned and cross-questioned Him, or perhaps, in order to understand Him better, allowed Him to take His place among them. At all events, the words of Holy Scripture point to an out-of-the-ordinary and striking situation, to a distinction shown the child that was unusual with the teaching authority of the synagogue (Luke 2:46–48). We may merely conjecture what the topic of discussion was — perhaps the advent of the Messiah. The fact is, this child caused a sort of revolution in the Temple synagogue. The ancient, semideified teaching staff of the law allows itself to be taught by a child and pays him unprecedented marks of honor. Was not this a profoundly significant prophecy of the things that would come to pass?

It may have been just at this juncture that Joseph and Mary entered the hall and in wonder witnessed the scene. Mary, still under the reaction of her sorrow, although full of joy at the discovery of her beloved child, cried out to Him: "Son! Why hast Thou done so to us? Thy father and I have sought Thee sorrowing." Our Savior arose and answered in an earnest and majestic voice: "Did you not know that I must be about my Father's business?"

(Luke 2:48–49). A sublime dignity radiated from His whole being, so that His parents kept silence and marveled in reverential awe. Jesus, however, accompanied His parents through the silent throng and with them set forth on His return journey to Nazareth.

How natural it was for Mary's sensitive heart to give expression to those grief-burdened words! It appears, however, that Joseph, the observant and reflecting man and father, remained silent and uttered not a word. He pondered in his heart the mystery underlying the occurrence. And it was a profound mystery for Jesus thus to leave His parents secretly, to cause them such bitter sorrow and excruciating anxiety in the very midst of the life of obedience and submission, which up to this He had been leading, and then to appear so suddenly in the Temple and to distinguish Himself so brilliantly in the midst of the life of humility and obscurity in which He had hid Himself.

This mystery is a prelude of His Messianic vocation and of His public life, a revelation of His divinity amid peculiar circumstances of poverty and detachment from all things, indeed, as some of the Fathers of the Church say, a foreshadowing even of His death and three days' burial.[4]

The association of Saint Joseph with this Messianic calling of Jesus is pointed to and brought out in clear light in various ways. He has a share in this vocation in his capacity of legal father. Thus, Mary gives him the preference and mentions him in the first place. He is, however, no more than a legal parent; for our Lord, in His answer to His Blessed Mother, contrasts him with another Father, to hear whom is His first, His higher vocation. Saint Joseph's position as regards the Messianic calling is further

---

[4] Saint Ambrose, *Expos. Evangel. sec. Lucam* II, 42, no. 63.

shown by his cooperation with the same, and particularly in his grief and anguish of heart.

Mary, Joseph, and even the Savior Himself are all in this mystery victims of this vocation. The sword of Simeon, which was to pierce Mary on Mount Calvary, even now makes its keenness felt in the heart of Joseph. Yet Joseph's connection with our Savior's Messianic mission affords him joy and honor, too. For this mystery is a glorious, most winning revelation of the Savior because personally made by Him for the first time, and because it is a manifestation of His divine wisdom and amiability, which are here so striking that even the conceited, proud, and stiff-necked doctors of the law forget themselves and publicly pay their homage to our Lord in the Temple. What an honor and joy for Saint Joseph to be the father of such a Child and the representative of the heavenly Father! And thus the overwhelming sorrow of Saint Joseph ends in unexpected joy and honor.

Chapter 8

⌒

The Life of Saint Joseph at Nazareth

After this ever memorable Paschal festival, fraught with the keenest suffering, the life of Saint Joseph henceforward was illumined by the clear, cheering sunshine of peace and happiness. This sunlight is the so-called hidden life at Nazareth. Whatever the holy Gospels mention regarding our divine Savior concerns Saint Joseph also. We shall endeavor to collect these various characteristic traits, so as to form a picture of our saint during this hidden life.

Nazareth, the circumscribed scene of action of this period, is nestled in its homelike charm in a small valley of the northern heights of the plain of Esdraelon. The fortresslike houses of the town rise in picturesque irregularity, one above the other, on a declivity of a mount situated to the north, from which a splendid view unfolds itself over the plain of Esdraelon, toward Mount Carmel, the Mediterranean, and northward, even as far as snow-capped Hermon. The landscape of Nazareth itself presents no jagged towering peaks or wild forest solitudes. Nazareth is synonymous with seclusion and calm earnestness, therefore wholly representative of an ordinary workaday existence, as befits the mystery of the hidden life.

The Truth About Saint Joseph

The houses of the Orient are usually square in form, constructed of stone and clay, and coated with lime. Above the few living rooms on the ground floor projects the upper story, or terrace, connected by a staircase with the courtyard. The latter is enclosed by a wall or a fence, and as a rule contains a bake oven and a grapevine or a fig tree. Thus, too, the home of Saint Joseph and of the Holy Family may have been arranged. It seems that a part of the dwelling was hewn in a rock, and the front portion was built of stone. Here, then, Saint Joseph spent the quiet, happy years of the hidden life with Jesus and Mary.

Holy Scripture, as we have seen, makes particular mention of the fact that the parents of Jesus every year journeyed to Jerusalem for the celebration of the Pasch (Luke 2:42). This is an indication of the life of piety and prayer Saint Joseph led with his family. The daily life of a Jewish family was preeminently religious. At the very door, just inside the house, where a holy-water font would be in a Christian home, was fastened a little wooden receptacle in which strips of parchment containing texts of the law were kept and reverently touched by all who entered or departed. The domestic devotions were supplemented by the religious exercises of the synagogue. In every village, there was a synagogue, which possessed a sort of choir, somewhat elevated above the congregation. Here was the veiled niche containing the sacred scrolls, and here too were the seats of honor for the scribes and the lectors. In these assembly halls the Sacred Scripture was read and explained, prayers were recited in common, and petitions were sent up to Heaven for the coming of the Messiah. These services were held on weekdays also.

At night the father of the family was accustomed to assemble the members under the large house lamp for community prayers. Thus, without stretching the imagination too far, we may suppose that Saint Joseph, after his day's toil, took the divine Child on his knee, recited for Him texts of Scripture and prayers, raised Him in his arms on their leaving the house that He might kiss the little receptacle containing the parchment strips of the law, and in due time brought Him to the synagogue and chanted the psalms with Him. Later on, too, when our Savior, like other children, had outgrown His school years and had become a young man, He may well have been accustomed with profound wisdom and charming modesty to explain at the evening home circle the texts of Scripture that had been publicly read in the synagogue. His words, in the case of Mary and Joseph, fell on good soil and brought forth in these privileged hearts fruit a thousandfold. Such in a measure was their life of piety.

It is, moreover, repeatedly mentioned in Holy Writ that Saint Joseph was a carpenter (Matt. 13:55; Mark 6:3). Hence, his life with his family was one of toil. While the Mother of God attended to the household duties — spun, sewed, made the necessary small purchases, every morning and evening procured water from the well, and prepared the family meals — Saint Joseph labored at his trade in the workshop. There was no room for lordly indolence or Asiatic dreaminess in this family. No one in this home wished to eat bread that he had not diligently earned.

In due time, too, as soon as His age and strength permitted it, our Divine Savior began to help His foster father in his work. It was now that the blessed years of the master tradesman began for Saint Joseph, by his introducing the youthful Christ into his apprenticeship. For labor, be it not forgotten, formed part of the life's program for the God-Man. What a heavenly happiness for Saint Joseph thus to work at the side of his divine apprentice, while he led and directed Him! He guided the Savior's hand, prepared His work, and with solicitous eye watched His efforts.

The Truth About Saint Joseph

We may surmise that his heart overflowed with sentiments of reverence, love, adoration, and joy as his sturdy hand rested on that of the Christ Child. Yet no emotion betrayed itself in his amiable, recollected, and quiet bearing. He acted in all simplicity and familiarity, as though accustomed from eternity to be the instructor of the Incarnate God. The diligence, earnestness, and perseverance of his divine disciple, whose boyish hands gradually hardened under the toil, stimulated Saint Joseph to even greater assiduity in his own labors, now that they received a sublime value from their participation in the work of the Redemption.

After the hours of labor followed the family repast, at which the thought that the divine Child was being supported by the toil of his hands must have been a touching consolation to Saint Joseph. On the Sabbath days, after the services of the synagogue, Joseph must surely have been accustomed to take the Child of his heart for a walk to the hilltops of Nazareth, and in the charming view stretching out before them to point out stately Mount Hermon in the north with Caesarea Philippi at its foot, then the vicinity where the lovely Lake of Gennesaret lies sequestered with the neighboring towns of Capernaum, Bethsaida, and Magdala, lastly the Plain of Esdraelon with the city of Nain and in the direction of beautiful Mount Carmel, the wide expanse of the Mediterranean. These names certainly made an impression on the thoughtful boy, who tarried in spirit with the souls that were awaiting His coming and reflected on the wonderful works He would there accomplish. But all this was still hidden from Saint Joseph's vision.

Another point in the hidden life of our Lord emphatically referred to by Holy Writ is the fact that in His youth He was ever subject to His parents (Luke 2:51). We cannot conceive His acting otherwise than obeying so readily, cheerfully, and promptly, and so conforming Himself to all their wishes and directions that it appeared nothing could afford Him greater pleasure than to receive orders and instructions. He was divine wisdom and holiness itself; and yet unnoticed, but steadily, He developed externally to boyhood, and from boyhood to adolescent manhood. This naturally leads us to the consideration of the wise, mild, quiet, and fatherly government of Saint Joseph in the midst of the Holy Family, the head of which he was. Assuredly he made but a moderate use of his authority. He gave few commands. In general, in a well-regulated family there is little room for commands. The regulations of the home serve as a standing order; the rest is read in the eyes of the parents. So, too, when Saint Joseph's authority was exercised, it was done in all humility. It has already been remarked that authority makes people humble. Who had a better heart than Joseph? His authority, moreover, extended to God and the Mother of God. Again, no one commands better than he who obeys exactly. Joseph was a man of perfect obedience and submissiveness to all properly constituted authority, but above all to God. And thus his orders were rather requests, and the execution of his plans were for the most part undertaken by himself that he might not have to command. He ministered to others rather than was ministered to. Hence, quiet, peace, contentment, harmony, joy, and love held sway in his glorious little realm, as in the peaceful and happy abode of Heaven itself, thanks to the tact and humble love of the governing master of the house.

Finally, Holy Scripture twice recalls the fact that our Savior grew and waxed strong, was full of wisdom, and found grace before God and men — that He increased in wisdom, age, and grace before God and men (Luke 2:40, 52). These words afford us a glimpse into the interior life of Saint Joseph, that is, into the effects that the continual sight of and association with our divine Savior produced in his heart. Even the daily intimate company of Mary, that chosen one of all creatures, whose mere appearance, action, and speech were manifestations of the highest virtue and holiness, and radiated grace and attracted to virtue, was in itself sufficient to sanctify the heart of any mortal.

Mary, however, was only the Mother of God; our Savior was God Himself. And this divine Person revealed Himself to Joseph in the most charming and amiable manner, in the guise of a Child, in whose regard he fulfilled the part of father, and with whom he continually lived in the most intimate familiarity. It was Saint Joseph's enviable privilege, then, to care for and nurture this Child with the solicitude of a father; it was his to observe the beautiful mystery of the Child's development; to notice how His features became ever more pronounced and expressive; how His wisdom ever more and more lovably manifested itself; how He advanced to more perfect ways and, finally, progressed from boyhood to youth, from youth to the perfection of manhood. Our saint had the opportunity daily and hourly to study His countenance, the bright mirror of divine beauty and wisdom and of all the mysteries of God, in the various manifestations of human life, in the exterior unconsciousness of His childish slumber, in the glowing expression of His joy and love, in the ecstasy of His devotion and contemplation. Just as the angels in wonder and adoration, with unlimited desire for knowledge and unquenchable ardor of love, are held enraptured by the vision of God, so did our saint gather all his thoughts and the impulses of his heart in this focal point of all beauty, the countenance of the Incarnate God. What mysteries were not disclosed to him in this vision!

If it is related of Mary "that she kept all these words, pondering them in her heart" (Luke 2:19), and this seems to be the whole content of her life, we may readily suppose the same of Saint Joseph. He directed all his concerns to Jesus, the living, visible, and only center of his life. This Savior was his foster son, his God, his supreme happiness of soul; his knowledge of Him and love of Him were his soul's one occupation, service, rest, and bliss. They were indeed the sum and substance of his whole life, certainly the most charming and most sublime, the only worthy preoccupation of the life of one who possessed the unheard of dignity and prerogative of being so near to the Savior and of even having the name and exercising the office of father of Jesus.

It is quite true that the life of Saint Joseph and of his Holy Family, as regards the exterior, was an ordinary, modest, unassuming life, and, we may say, a life of monotonous poverty. But what treasures of genuine peace and of true joy were hidden in its interior! In this realm no one wished to be in command or give orders, but all desired from a motive of humble love rather to obey and serve one another. And where love reigns supreme, there are peace and joy, but only there.

Chapter 9

⁂

The Death of Saint Joseph

The confidingly peaceful happiness of the life at Nazareth was interrupted by the death of Saint Joseph, which occurred a considerable number of years after the ever memorable Paschal festival. We have no certain information about either the time or the circumstances of his passing. It appears that Saint Joseph was no longer alive when our Lord, in about His thirtieth year, left Nazareth to begin His public life. We do not find him among the guests of Cana, a sign that he was absent from the celebration and undoubtedly was already dead. His name would otherwise have been mentioned, seeing that Jesus and the Mother of Jesus were among the number of those who had been invited. So, too, he was not among the loyal-hearted souls who surrounded the Cross of Jesus on the hill of Calvary; otherwise our dying Savior would not have commended His Blessed Mother to the care of Saint John. We may be allowed to suppose that his death took place after our Lord had advanced to maturer manhood and was Himself in a position to provide for His mother. Hence, of the grandeur of our Savior's public activities, the saint witnessed nothing. He could have only an inkling of the same from reading the prophets, and perhaps from the confidential disclosures of our Lord Himself.

As Moses viewed the Promised Land from Mount Nebo, so our saint greeted at a distance the glorious earthly career of his divine Son. And, as later on Saint John the Baptist vanished from the scene in favor of the Master, so according to the designs of Divine Providence did Saint Joseph make room for our Lord after having fulfilled the office of foster father, teacher, and protector of Christ's youth. Indeed, how could he under different arrangements have borne the sad culmination of the Master's glorious public appearance, the hatred and persecution of the Jews, and finally, the shocking end of his heart's own Son and of his God?

Uncertain as are the time and place of our saint's death, so, too, are its precise circumstances. Whether he enjoyed with Jesus and Mary the privilege of immunity from the inconveniences and burdens of personal sickness and was subjected only to the general indispositions of nature, as fatigue and death, who will say? It is generally assumed that he died from some sickness or other, indeed, but still more from the magnitude and depth and stress of his love for his Son and his God. For we have seen how exceptionally privileged, even unique, were the office and relationship of our saint with respect to the God-Man, and how under such circumstances an altogether superabundant measure of every virtue, and especially of love, must have accumulated in his spotless, holy, and loyal father's heart. Of a truth he was the palm that graced the courts of the Lord, the cypress tree of Zion, ever rejoicing in the sight of the Holy of Holies, the tree of paradise that flourished along the running waters of eternal life, drawing its very life's vigor directly from the divine fountainhead. For God is grateful; and if our Savior heaped so many blessings on the shepherds, the Magi, Simeon, John the Baptist, and others because they greeted His grace-giving presence with appreciative hearts for a brief passing hour, how much more did He bless Saint Joseph, who had sanctified himself for so many years in the immediate company of our Lord by the most intimate and confidential relations and the closest association with Him. If our Lord regards every cup of water and every corporal and spiritual work of mercy, performed on behalf of our fellow men out of love for Him, as done to Himself, and promises Heaven as a reward, what must have been the extent of His gratitude to Joseph, who, in the truest sense of the word, had received Him, given Him shelter, clothed, nourished, and consoled Him, had served Him with all conceivable solicitude, at the sacrifice of his strength and rest, amid untold difficulties and privations, and with a love that transcended the love of all fathers and of all mankind?

God really and personally made Himself Saint Joseph's debtor. And so it behooved our divine Master to repay His debt of gratitude by an unceasing inpouring of graces, and preeminently the grace of an increase of love, which is the best and most perfect of all gifts. In this manner our saint's heart became an abyss of love, the ardor and the craving, surging flood of which the frail form of his body and delicate web of his life could not long resist. This child, his own God, really drew out and exhausted our saint's vigor of life by the impelling force of love. The more the charming childlikeness and amiability of our Lord's youth merged into the meekness, calm earnestness, and majesty of His manhood, the more did the love of our saint retreat into his innermost soul and with surer insistence undermine his life until, yielding to its irresistible power and importunity, his body lost all resistance and collapsed, while his soul followed the triumphant upward impulse of its love and winged its flight from earth.

The Truth About Saint Joseph

It was eminently fitting that at the departure of his beloved foster-parent out of this life, the love and gratitude of his son should assert their generosity and help to render his death most beautiful, edifying, lovable, and consoling. So it was. The Lord of life who bears not only our bodies, but our souls, too, in the hollow of His hand, sustaining and strengthening them, and who by the interior workings of His grace can change the most bitter circumstance of our lives, that of approaching death, into a paradise of consolation and bliss, stood at the bedside of the dying father and spouse with Mary, the sweetness and hope of all mankind; and they supported and held him in their loving arms. The only thing that might possibly have been a source of regret to the departing soul of the holy foster father was the privation of personal association with Jesus. Yet how soon was the parting to be transformed into the joy of reunion amid the glory of the resurrection day. And the verdict of the judge, which was in keeping with such a life's close, was a kiss of grateful affection from his divine foster Son as our saint breathed forth his liberated soul into the blissful realms beyond. The cheering word that the Lord will speak to all His righteous servants: "Well done, thou good and faithful servant, enter thou into the joy of thy Lord" (Matt. 25:21), and the consoling assurance which at a future moment a poor contrite sinner, the good thief, would receive from the mouth of our dying Master, "This day thou shalt be with me in paradise" (Luke 23:43), must surely with far greater right have been the parting consolation from the Son to his foster father. Thus may we imagine the death of Saint Joseph to have been. Antiquity has left us no description of the hallowed event. Credit for this is due to more recent Christian art.

The transfigured soul of the saint appeared like a luminously consoling dawn upon the vision of the holy forefathers and prophets and patriarchs sojourning in the expectant twilight of Limbo and conveyed to them the glad tidings of the advent of the Redeemer. But where was the venerable and holy body of the saint buried? Was it under the peaceful cypresses at Nazareth, or in Jerusalem, where later on the Savior and, as tradition has it, the Mother of God had their place of burial? We have no definite information on this matter. In the latter supposition the three hearts which on earth had loved one another so intensely and were inseparable would have shared together their last resting place.

Part 2

Saint Joseph in the
Life of the Church

Introduction to Part 2

The real life of Saint Joseph, or his active relationship to the person of his divine foster Son on earth, closed with the death of the saint. He still continues, however, a sort of afterlife here below in the Church, which is the Mystical Body of Christ. The grounds for such abiding activity are his great dignity, the example of his virtues, and the power of his intercession and protection. By means of these the saint exerts his encouraging, purifying, sanctifying, and consoling influence throughout the various parts of the Church, and inspires the faithful to venerate him and imitate his exalted virtues.

Sublime indeed, extraordinary, and in keeping with his high dignity and merits as well as with the gratitude and generosity of his divine foster Son, is the saint's heavenly glory. The measure of his service during his earthly sojourn was that of his unbounded love. Hence, our divine Master repays him now with a full measure of glory, a measure pressed down and shaken together and flowing over (Luke 6:38). He has placed His good and faithful servant over all His goods (Matt. 24:47), and has set up the throne of His adoptive father next to that of His purest Mother. The grandeur of the saint's glory, however, is at present hidden from our view and comprehension but will one day, to our supreme joy, be revealed to us in a happy eternity. Still, a reflection of the greatness of his glory manifests itself here below precisely in his activity in the Church's kingdom, which itself is the counterpart of God's kingdom beyond. And from the extent of his influence on earth, we may in a manner obtain a concept of what Saint Joseph's meed of honor, power, and joy must be in the supernal realms of bliss.

We shall then, to the best of our ability, try to gain an insight into Saint Joseph's influence upon earth and into the reverence and love shown him by the faithful. Let us start with the marks of honor and dignity that are paid to his person by reason of his relationship to the God-Man, Christ Jesus, and that throw such a vivid light on the greatness of his virtues, fill the devout faithful with veneration for him, and urge them to a zealous imitation of him.

Chapter 10

The Shadow of the Heavenly Father

Spiritual writers are fond of calling Saint Joseph the shadow of the heavenly Father, an engaging, elevated, and truthful representation indeed. It expresses the full extent of his greatness and the complete concept of his high vocation in a most concise and sublime manner. Above all, he was the foster father of the Savior. The heavenly Father is the type and origin of all fatherhood in Heaven and on earth (Eph. 3:15); and so every human father is a representative and image of the heavenly Father. In the case of Saint Joseph, however, this is verified in a most characteristic and glorious manner, and that from three viewpoints.

First, Saint Joseph is the image of the heavenly Father as regards authority. Authority is the first distinguishing mark of the father. It is naught else than one's power and right to govern and command because one is either the originator of life or occupies a position of superiority, which in a way is also a kind of original authorship, for no society can come into being or continue in existence without a head. Each of these kinds of authority has its origin and type in the heavenly Father, who in the Godhead Itself represents the principle of origin, destiny, and conservation.

The Truth About Saint Joseph

This fatherhood is the august distinction and the glory of the first Person of the Most Holy Trinity. The eternal Father condescends to transfer His royal right to Saint Joseph, and this in a manner not granted to any other man. True, Saint Joseph is not the natural father of the Savior. Because of his marriage bond with Mary, however, he is the head of the Holy Family, and all its members are by right subject to him. The divine Master Himself, because of His generation from the Father, says that He is less than the Father (John 14:28); He is subject to the saint by reason of the saint's position of authority as head of the Holy Family. Jesus belongs to Joseph as foster son, and this relationship is always recognized by the heavenly Father. Saint Joseph confers the name of Jesus upon the Child; he presents Him in the Temple to the heavenly Father; to Joseph the heavenly Father makes known the commands and directions for the guidance of the Holy Family.

The divine Savior and Mary also saw in Joseph the visible representative of the heavenly Father. This was the reason why our Lord, as a young man, and perhaps even as a man, was subject to Joseph and carried out his orders with so much readiness, with such prompt, joyful obedience, and with such perseverance. In Joseph the Savior saw the shadow of the glory of His eternal Father; in the direction of the saint He recognized the will of His heavenly Father; in His converse with Joseph He held, in a manner, converse with His own heavenly Father; and while obeying the saint, He could always say: "For I do always the things that please Him" (John 8:29). It cannot be denied that this perfect obedience of Jesus to Joseph, lasting for so many years, is a glorification of the saint's fatherhood simply unsurpassed. The more profound and the more prolonged the humility of Jesus, practiced in regard to Joseph, the greater the dignity and the elevation of the saint.

The Shadow of the Heavenly Father

The comparison of Saint Joseph's fatherhood with that of the heavenly Father discloses to us another glorious characteristic. The eternal Father begot His Son from all eternity in perfect sanctity and purity. What can be fancied purer and more spiritual than the origin of thought or of an idea in the faculty of our understanding? Such, in a manner, although infinitely purer and more wonderful, is the eternal generation of the only-begotten Son of the Father. The Father knows Himself and, in this knowledge of self, begets the living and substantial Image and Word of His divine nature. This living Image of His glory is His Son.

A similar mark of purity characterizes the fatherhood of Saint Joseph. Natural fatherhood has an advantage and a disadvantage. Its advantage lies in the actual conferring of human nature and life on the child; its disadvantage is in the fact that it sacrifices virginity and bodily integrity. The divine nature of the heavenly Father and the Son, as well as the predictions of the prophets, demanded that our Savior should not have a natural father during His sojourn on earth, but only a natural mother. Hence, as our Faith teaches us, Saint Joseph is not the natural parent, but merely the legal father of the Redeemer. Without its being on this account a mere empty title, the fatherhood of Saint Joseph embraces the glory of virginal integrity, and thus lays claim to a new mark of resemblance to the Fatherhood of God. The heavenly Father has given to the saint's fatherhood all that He could without detriment to his virginity. Moreover, the fatherhood of Saint Joseph resembles that of the eternal Father because both have but one Son, in fact, the same Son. How admirably and gloriously the fatherhood of the saint shines forth in comparison with that of the first Person of the Blessed Trinity! Because of his virginal fatherhood, artists frequently depict Saint Joseph holding the lily in his hand.

The third mark of resemblance of Saint Joseph's fatherhood to that of God the Father is love. It was love, not nature, that made our saint the father of Christ. We love the concepts and ideas of our mind and intellect as our own property, indeed, as part of our very selves, since, in truth, nothing so closely claims our proprietorship as the creations of our own thought. In a similar way, God the Father comprehends with supreme complacence His only-begotten Son as the substantial, infinitely perfect, and infinitely lovable image of His nature and essence, and begets Him continually, according to the words of the Psalmist: "My son art Thou, this day have I begotten Thee" (Ps. 2:7). In fact, each time the voice of the eternal Father resounds from the cloud that hovers over the Savior, He calls Him His "well-beloved Son" (Matt. 3:17; Luke 9:35; 2 Pet. 1:17).

Joseph is indeed but the shadow of the heavenly Father; yet the accents of love that God the Father addressed to Christ through Joseph, His earthly representative, were not a lifeless sound, but such an expression of love from a heart of flesh and blood as no other father could have for his child. Once we grant that God wished to give His Son an earthly father, we cannot conceive His selecting any other than one possessed of the truest, deepest, sincerest love.

Hence, together with His authority He bestowed on Saint Joseph something of His infinite love for His divine Son; indeed, the measure of love bestowed amply compensated the saint for what was wanting in natural fatherhood. Just as God the Father, in giving Mary His Son, furnished her in a manner with His divine love, so, too, in due proportion did He favor Saint Joseph. The latter gave abundant proof of the greatness, depth, and intensity of his love, not only in words and feelings, but in deeds and toils and sacrifices of all sorts. The virginal purity of his fatherhood was no hindrance to his love; on the contrary, if ever a heart can be capable of and strong in love, it is a pure, virginal heart that, freed from all obstacles, mounts to God, the highest good. So strong in fact was the love in the heart of Saint Joseph that it is supposed to have eventually consumed his very life.

We see, then, that Saint Joseph is a sublime, venerable, amiable reflection of the eternal Father. His fatherhood is indisputably one of the most charming and lovely of God's thoughts, one of the most touching of God's manifestations to man. The divine Child in the fatherly arms of Saint Joseph is, as it were, the visible appearance of the unbegotten Father and the only-begotten Son, of the Son sent into this world and of the Father not sent. As regards Mary, divine motherhood was the condition and end of all her graces and privileges; and her motherhood, according to Saint Thomas,[5] belongs to the three objects or possibilities in which the almighty power of God exhausts itself. Nothing approaches this motherhood so closely as the fatherhood of Saint Joseph, to whom God Himself and His Mother were subject. In all the vast dwelling place of the heavenly Father, the sun and moon obey His call. Similarly, in the residence of Saint Joseph, Jesus, the Sun of Justice, and Mary, fair as the moon, obeyed his word. Saint Joseph alone could lay claim to this honor. Only for him has God the Father reserved this high dignity. "I am the Lord; I will not give my glory to another" (Isa. 42:8).

If something still can and ought to be added to this portrait of Saint Joseph, it should be done here. The saint is the representative of the heavenly Father. Above all, he is a father in the highest acceptance of the term. He is a father to our Savior;

---

[5] Saint Thomas Aquinas, *Summa Theologica*, I, Q. 25, art. 6, ad. 4.

to Mary, as regards his outward relationship to her, he is hardly more than a father. Therefore, his chief characteristic is his fatherhood, with all the qualities that adorn it: quiet of mind and reflection, unselfishness, faithfulness, and inexhaustible love. Thus, in the Gospel story we meet Saint Joseph as the very essence of imperturbable calm in the midst of all sorts of terrors, as the very presence of mind itself in exciting contingencies, as utter meekness and patience in torturing cares, as the very image of wonderful simplicity and unpretentiousness while adorned with the most signal marks of predilection and prerogatives of honor, as the most accommodating charity and unchangeable fortitude in the fulfillment of duty. By means of these admirable and attractive characteristics, the saint presents to us an image of the heavenly Father, who in the triune Godhead is the type of Divine Providence ruling from end to end calmly and mightily.

Chapter 11

⌒

The Saint of the Childhood of Jesus

Let us descend from the heavenly Father to His divine Son, whom He sent into the world and allowed to become man for us. Here we are face-to-face with the great mystery of the Incarnation, face-to-face with the God-Man, who is the occasion and the central object of this mystery. The relation of Saint Joseph to this mystery is summed up in two considerations—namely, what the saint has contributed to this mystery and how he contributed to it.

The saint shared in the mystery of the Incarnation in three ways.

First, he contributed in his own particular way to the realization of the Incarnation. As is known, he was not the natural father of Jesus. Thus, his relation to the Incarnation is not an immediate one. Mary alone was immediately connected with the actual fulfillment of the mystery, in that she gave her consent to Christ's conception and allowed the Holy Spirit to form the sacred humanity of Jesus from her blood. Only in an indirect manner did Saint Joseph participate in the mystery, by fulfilling the conditions dependent on him and necessary for the Incarnation—namely, the protection of Mary's virginity. It was of paramount necessity that the conception and birth of Christ should be virginal. This condition Saint Joseph fulfilled in faithfully safeguarding the virginity of his spouse before and during his married life with her.

Only a few condemners of virginity and destroyers of our Lord's honor have dared to deny this prerogative, contrary to the universal belief of Christians, by presenting a few less evident texts in a contrary sense (Matt. 1:25; 12:46). Sometimes Holy Writ mentions an occurrence that does not take place up to a certain point, without, however, intending to convey the meaning that it does occur later (Gen. 8:7; 49:10; Ps. 109:1). Thus, too, the word "brethren" in the Scripture is applied to all classes of kindred. Hence, when in the Sacred Text there is a reference to the brethren of Jesus (Matt. 12:47), the word may with equal right be applied to Joseph's brothers or sisters. Again, when Jesus is designated as the "firstborn," the phrase may properly mean the "only-begotten" son — that is, to the exclusion of any other. In fact, it often happens that the firstborn child is the only one born.

For us Catholics, belief in the undefiled and perpetual virginity of Mary has been firmly established by the watchword of the Church: "Mary, a virgin before the divine birth, at the divine birth, and after the divine birth." Saint Joseph respected and sacredly guarded the virginity of Mary. Therefore, he fulfilled the condition and brought to his marriage bond with Mary a disposition without which the Incarnation would not have taken place. This virginal marriage was, indeed, the final arrangement of God for the advent of the Savior, and Saint Joseph made it possible. He fulfilled not some merely indifferent condition in the realization of the Incarnation, but one that God from eternity had foreseen, willed, and decreed. The virginity of Saint Joseph was included as a cooperating agent in the eternal decree of God that determined the Incarnation. We have seen that at the espousals of Mary and Joseph a very special providence of God prevailed, the precise purposes of which were the virginity of this union and the advent of Jesus, who was to become incarnate dependent on the saint's virginity. We may therefore say with Saint Augustine, "Joseph is so much the more a father, the more virginal he is";[6] indeed, we may add, he is a father because a virgin. In this way and not otherwise did Joseph participate in the actual carrying out of the Incarnation.

Much more directly, indeed, in a manner much more effectual and excellent did the saint share in the support, upbringing, and safeguarding of the divine humanity. Jesus, this divine Child, had an infinitely wise, rich, powerful Father in Heaven. But this Father exercised His wisdom and love toward His Son by giving Him on earth a foster father who was to be to Him a support, a protector, and His all; and for this purpose He furnished Him with the genuine heart of a father, a heart full of love and self-sacrifice. But this father was a mortal man, Saint Joseph, who in his poverty could lay claim to nothing but the product of his hands. With the toil of his hands he was obliged to offer protection to God forsaken in this world, to procure for Him sustenance, clothing, and nourishment. It was to his care that this mysterious poor one, this Child, apparently fatherless on earth, was left. And when Herod sought the Child to put Him to death, the heavenly Father sent an angel indeed, but only as a messenger, giving orders for the flight; the rest He left entirely in the hands of the appointed protector. Then it was that the fatherly love of Joseph was the only stronghold that received and protected the

---

[6] Saint Augustine, *Sermo* 51, chap. 20, no. 30.

divine Child—the fatherly love of the saint, which carried the Child through the desert into the land of the pharaohs and there concealed Him carefully until all His enemies were removed. Then, on the arms of Joseph, the Child returned to the Holy Land to be nurtured and provided for at Nazareth during many years by the labor of the saint's hands. This support and upbringing of the Child is mentioned in Holy Writ by merely one word; yet it expresses in truth, according to the ordinary measure of human life, a duration of days, weeks, and years. Whatever a human son owes to a human father for all the benefits of his rearing and support, Jesus owes to Joseph. He was to Jesus a foster father, teacher, and protector—in a word, His all, here below.

A third aspect of the saint's participation in the mystery of the Incarnation regards the application of the effects, blessings, and graces of the Incarnation to mankind. This is the solicitude of the saint in regard to Christ's Mystical Body, which is made up of the faithful, and without which we cannot even adequately consider Christ. He came into the world and assumed human nature only for the purpose of making of us His Mystical Body and of uniting us by means of grace to Himself as our head. This Mystical Body is, as it were, the spiritual extension of Christ become incarnate, whom Saint Joseph nurtured and educated with fatherly love. The purpose and end of this education was none other than ourselves. The angel gave sufficient evidence of this fact when he told Joseph to confer on the Child the name of Jesus because He would save His people from their sins, would redeem them actually and efficaciously through grace, the very source of which is the great mystery of the Incarnation. Saint Joseph continually carries on this mystery and is its devoted servant by procuring graces for us from his Son, as we shall have occasion to see in greater detail directly. "Four things," says a spiritual writer, "caused our downfall: a woman, a man, a tree, and a serpent; four things restored us again: Mary, Christ, the Cross, and Joseph."

Moreover, Joseph above all rendered his services to the divine humanity with a singular love. The less the saint had to do in a bodily manner toward effecting the Incarnation, the more was this omission to be compensated for by love if he would properly administer his office. God attended to that. When Divine Providence bestows a mission on anyone, it also grants him the necessary means and qualifications. God creates the hearts of men (Ps. 32:15); He can change them and mold them like wax, and direct them as watercourses. And, as on a later occasion, at the Master's word to John, "Behold thy mother" (John 19:27), the evangelist, to do justice to his charge, was given a son's heart toward Mary like unto the Savior's heart, so did God the Father direct the heart of Joseph to the Child Jesus by sympathy, cooperation, and fatherly love. This was a heavenly supernatural love in the heart of Joseph, a love far deeper and more powerful than any natural father's love could be.

Furthermore, Joseph served the humanity of Jesus with great unselfishness, without any regard to self-interest, but not without sacrifices and inconveniences. He does not toil for himself but seems to be an instrument intended for the benefit of others, an instrument that is put aside as soon as it has done its work, and this apparently without recognition. In fact, Saint Joseph appears in the Gospel story only in connection with the Child Jesus and disappears from the scene once the childhood of Christ has passed. Of the great and sublime mysteries of the childhood of Christ, of which he was a witness and which were so honorable and glorious to him, hardly a ray falls upon Saint Joseph.

On the contrary, it is the particular vocation of the saint to dim the divine light of the mysteries, to hide them, and thereby to withdraw himself from notice. He is the shadow of the heavenly Father not only in the sense that he is the earthly representative of the authority of God the Father as regards the Son; but also by means of his apparent natural fatherhood he is to conceal for a while the divinity of this Son. This beautiful and amiable Child, whom Saint Joseph carries in his arms, has God in Heaven as Father and is Himself God. This is a great light; and if this light shines with all its brightness upon the Child, its beams fall upon the whole earth with the effulgent glory of the divinity. This, however, was not to take place immediately.

Hence, by means of his foster fatherhood God places Saint Joseph as a shadow between Himself and the Christ Child; and this shadow so conceals the light that, if we except a few faint rays, the bright side of the divine mystery remains hidden and for Joseph, too, produces no results. This is certainly a wonderfully sublime and divine vocation, but not the most welcome to human nature. Such, then, are the relations of the saint to the humanity of Jesus.

These relations are so intimate and important that, with the exception of the Mother of Jesus, no one else can claim them. The mystery of the Incarnation, however, is of the highest, yes, of the most fundamental importance to the Church and Christendom; and to this mystery the life of the saint is immediately dedicated. He is truly the angel of the great council and the saint of the holy childhood of Jesus, its protector and nurturer—the living, created providence, we might say, which watches over the Christ Child. Such is the peculiar greatness and glory of Saint Joseph's vocation. It proves that his is a very special and signal rank among the saints of the Kingdom of God. For in the various arrangements of the natural and supernatural worlds and in the different communications of God to His creatures, there exists one order that surpasses in dignity and holiness every other order of nature and of grace. This is the hypostatic order or the circle, whose center and focus is the humanity of Jesus in its personal union with the second Person of the Divinity.

The luminaries revolving about and serving the central sun are the saints who have participated in the realization of the mystery of the Incarnation and who thus form a special relationship to the God-Man and are linked to His person by a most intimate union. All other saints, as great as they may be, are connected with a mission of Christ, but those just referred to are directly concerned with His person. To this privileged class belong the distinguished family of blood relations of our Lord and God; and hence Saint Joseph in a most special manner, not only because he is the nearest and the last of David's descendants, but also because he is the husband of Mary and the legal father of the Savior. No one except Mary, the Mother of Jesus according to the flesh, can dispute our saint's rank in this class. Such is Saint Joseph's position in the Kingdom of God, surpassing far in dignity and honor all the angels; for "to which of the angels did God say: Thou art my son?" (Heb. 1:5).

This dignity and honor assure the saint a very special degree of recognition, veneration, love, and gratitude from the hearts of all the members of Christ's kingdom. He is not only a powerful and great saint in the Kingdom of God, but a benefactor of the whole of Christendom and mankind. The benefactions of the Egyptian Joseph toward his family and people can in no manner be compared with those of Saint Joseph in regard to the Christian family. In the house of Joseph at Nazareth and under his care was the redemption of mankind prepared. What he accomplished he did for us; we are of a certainty the objective of all his undertakings.

Chapter 12

᷐

The Husband of Mary

In Holy Scripture special emphasis is given to the fact that Saint Joseph was the husband of Mary: "Jacob begot Joseph, the husband of Mary, of whom was born Jesus, who is called Christ" (Matt. 1:16). And this was but right. From this circumstance the weightiest consequences result for Saint Joseph, above all, his relationship to Mary, which was threefold.

First, the saint is the husband, the spouse, of Mary by his marriage contract with her. Holy Writ bears incontrovertible witness to this marriage (Matt. 1:16, 24; Luke 1:27; 2:48). All the holy Fathers and Doctors see in this union a true, genuine, and perfect marriage; and this because of the words of Holy Scripture and also because of the fact that all the conditions of a matrimonial contract are verified—namely, the mutual surrender of each to the other to lead a wedded life, the spiritual meaning of the marriage bond, which typifies the union of Christ with His Church (Eph. 5:32), and, finally, the blessing of a progeny. This nuptial contract is a great happiness to the saint, an extraordinary honor, and the foundation of untold advantages. Matrimony is the closest union that can exist among human beings here below. It produces not

only a union of bodies (Gen. 2:24; Matt. 19:5) but, much more, a
spiritual union of heart, of mind, and of love—an exchange of all
goods and qualities on the basis of friendship and similarity. The
Apostle says: "The man is the head of the woman" (1 Cor. 11:3).
Mary really belonged to Joseph with all she was and possessed. No
other person so possessed her esteem, subjection, and love. This
union not only brought Saint Joseph into daily familiar association with Mary, whose like could not be found among creatures,
but it was his privilege to behold continually her array of virtues
and share with her a mutual exchange of spiritual goods. Finally,
there were the reality, truth, honor, and happiness of being father
to the Savior. This fatherhood, the providential task and official
position of Saint Joseph in the Kingdom of God, has its true and
particular foundation in a special way in the matrimonial union
with Mary. Without this marriage the fatherhood of Joseph would
be a kind of adoptive fatherhood, by reason of the adoption of a
child; but on account of his marriage with Mary, Joseph is infinitely more the father of Jesus, a true, real, and legal father; and
he is acknowledged such before God and men, just because, by
reason of his union with Mary, a perfect, juridical exchange of
goods between man and wife is effected.

Whatever Mary had possessed belonged by right to Saint
Joseph also, by reason of a community of goods; and hence, this
included her Son, even though the latter had been given to her
by God in a wonderful way. Jesus belonged to Joseph as his legal
father. Yes, we may go even further and say that just as without
this marriage much would be lacking in the reality and truth
of the fatherhood of Saint Joseph, so without it, in the present
order of things, Mary would not have become the Mother of
God. According to God's decree, the marriage between Joseph
and Mary was the way in which the introduction of Christ into

the world was to be accomplished. The nuptial union of Saint Joseph with Mary was therefore really a great divine mystery, from which all benefits were to come to us.

Secondly, Saint Joseph is not only the husband of Mary, but also the protector and witness of her virginity. This mutual virginity of Joseph and Mary, just as in the case of their nuptial union, belonged essentially to the divine plan of the Incarnation, as we have already seen. It behooved Saint Joseph to be both the husband of Mary and the protector of her virginity, as he was in fact. In this sense an illustrious orator says that Joseph and Mary mutually presented their virginity to each other that it might be mutually protected;[7] and their matrimonial fidelity consisted in this, that they were to protect their virginity. This marriage was decreed by God in view of the conception and birth of Jesus; and hence, Saint Joseph had to espouse the Mother of God, who as such was to remain a virgin according to the prophecies, that thus the temporal birth of the Son of God without a father should be a sublime and wonderful representation of His eternal generation without a mother.

Mary and Joseph were like two stars, whose pure rays merged into one, to shine in the presence of God with the much more brilliant luster of an entirely divine purpose and appointment. Thus, this marriage more than any other fulfilled the sublime, mystical purpose of matrimony — namely, to be by its purity a faithful image of Christ's union with mankind and His Church. Saint Joseph, however, not only venerated and protected the Blessed Virgin, but was, too, in her regard, a witness and a refuge

---

[7] Jacques-Bénigne Bossuet, *Oeuvres*, III (Paris: Firmin Didot Fréres, 1841), 413.

beyond the shadow of suspicion just because of his nuptial bond with Mary.

The only reason Saint Joseph hesitated to take unto himself Mary his wife was the perplexity in his mind as to how motherhood and virginity could be united in his spouse. This perplexity moved Heaven to intervene in a wonderful way. For now an angel appeared to Joseph and put him at his ease by explaining everything. By means of this divine revelation, the saint himself became the unimpeachable witness of Mary's virginity. This was precisely God's purpose in the painful episode, to produce in Joseph a truly sublime witness to Mary's integrity. The Fathers of the Church always refer to this testimony in defending Mary's virginity.

Thus, Saint Joseph, like the cherub of old, stands guard with a flaming sword near the paradise of his spouse's virginity, a new reason for Mary's gratitude to and love for Joseph, her husband and virginal spouse. Mary is especially styled the "Spouse of the Holy Spirit," not merely by the power of sanctifying grace, the possession of which placed her in the position of spouse of the Holy Spirit, but because the Holy Spirit effected the Incarnation in her and through her. In this higher sense the Holy Spirit is in a unique way the Spouse of Mary, while Joseph, without ceasing to be Mary's spouse, is the "friend of the bridegroom."

How marvelous! Wherever anything great is to be accomplished, we find purity and virginity. Without it nothing exalted happens in the supernatural order. God will not become incarnate without it! The child of God is in a measure the blossom and fruit of virginity. There must be something singularly beautiful in virginal purity! It goes forth from God, allures God to earth, and unites the divine nature with the human. According to the Fathers of the Church, virginity is something in the flesh but not of the flesh, something spiritual, angelic, indeed, a reflection in man of the eternal, infinite beauty. Wherever God sees it, He forgets the lowliness of our carnal and earthly nature. Hence God selects a virginal father and a virginal mother, and finds in them a paradise of pleasure precisely because of their purity and virginity.

The third relationship of Joseph to Mary again results from his quality of husband and spouse, and belongs to the purposes of a matrimonial contract. The principal end of matrimony is the procreation of children. This end was realized in the case of our saint in a higher and more wonderful manner through the virginal conception of our Savior. We have already treated of this mystery.

The second end of matrimony consists in the advantage of mutual association, and every sort of cooperation. Saint Joseph was the faithful, loving companion, support, and comforter of the Mother of God. Mary's life was intended to be that of God's Mother, of the Mother of the Savior, who came upon earth not to reign in the midst of honors and pleasures, but to redeem the world by toil, suffering, and the Cross. Mary's life, too, was arranged according to this pattern, and in it Saint Joseph was to be her support and help. And thus we meet the Holy Family, if not in extreme poverty, at least in such need that Mary and Joseph were obliged to toil with their royal hands for their daily sustenance and that of the Christ Child; we find them on journeys just because of this child, fleeing in torturing perplexity from powerful persecutors into a strange, heathen country. This demanded decisive help, persevering action, and unfaltering courage. All these the delicate mother and virgin found in Saint Joseph. He was her guide and leader, her staff and support. Just as the People of Israel of old journeyed through the desert under the protection of the "pillar of cloud," so the Holy Family travel from Nazareth to Jerusalem, to Bethlehem, and as far as the land of Egypt, under the guidance and protection of faithful Saint Joseph. This is why the old mosaics invariably represent the saint with a staff in his hand; it is the symbol of guidance, protection, and defense.

How homelike, peaceful, and expressive of mutual love was the domestic life of the Holy Family in its willing submission to Saint Joseph's fatherly authority! The reason for this happy family life was the unlimited regard of the saint for Mary. A striking proof of this reverence and esteem of Joseph was the domestic perplexity that, as we have seen, immediately preceded their marriage. In fact, an ecclesiastical writer is of the opinion that the saint would rather have regarded the affair as a miracle than have admitted a suspicion in Mary's regard. How his esteem and veneration for the virgin must have increased when he learned that she was unsurpassedly holy and was even the Mother of God! His love for Mary, furthermore, was based upon this esteem for her. How every circumstance in the natural and supernatural order here combined to enhance this love for Mary in the heart of Joseph: the amiability and sanctity of his spouse, his own loving heart and intense realization of his responsibilities and God's holy will! Besides God and the divine Child, no one was so loved by Joseph as was Mary. Here, indeed, the Holy Spirit Himself was the bond of love that united both hearts.

From true love, peace and joy always arise. We have already seen how peaceful a character Saint Joseph was. Nothing disturbed the peace and happiness of this earthly sanctuary. Every extraneous suffering was hushed in the peace of the family circle and of their hearts, which recognized, wished, and sought nothing but the divine will. Even Jesus and Mary could find their edification in the calm, humble, and profound virtue, purity, and sanctity of Joseph. In the company of the divine Child and of her spouse, Mary no longer yearned for the courts of the Lord in Jerusalem, where, as a child of the Temple and a virgin, she had dedicated her youth to God and had mounted to such sublime heights of union with Him, the God of her heart. Here there was more than the Ark of the Covenant and more than the high priest! The happiest proof of how Joseph fulfilled all the duties and offices of husband and spouse toward Mary in accordance with God's plans; and to what extent his wisdom, holiness, and purity impressed the soul of Mary, this sublimest of all created beings; is the naturalness and easy grace and childlike confidence with which she submitted to Saint Joseph's guidance and could thus say with the spouse in the Canticle; "I sat down under His shadow, whom I desired" (Song of Sol. 2:3). Just as the Israelite in Solomon's time sat without fear, securely and trustfully, under his fig tree and vine, which nurtured him, so Jesus and Mary lived under the protection and loving care of Joseph.

This little chapter was intended to give but a faint image of the rich, beautiful, and sublime content of the words of Holy Writ, "Jacob begot Joseph, the husband of Mary, of whom was born Jesus, who is called Christ."

Chapter 13

⤙

The Man According to God's Own Heart

Another title of honor belonging to our saint is "the man according to God's own heart," "His right-hand man"—that is, the man of God's providence. This leads us more intimately into the relationship of Joseph with the Holy Spirit. Now, the Holy Spirit, because of His procession from the divine will or love, is the mutual, substantial love of the Father and the Son, or, typically expressed, the heart of the Holy Trinity. Hence, since nothing is more active than love, He is the principle of every activity properly ordered to its end. In a word, the Holy Spirit is the principle directing all things to an end, and all created beings must follow Him if they wish to arrive happily at their eternal goal. The Holy Spirit, the "Finger of God," who in His Wisdom drew forth all creatures from nothing, guides them to their end by His providence, in showing them their destiny and giving them the means to reach it. Every office and vocation and every happy fulfillment of a vocation proceeds from the Holy Spirit.

Saint Joseph, as foster father of Jesus and head of the Holy Family, had an exalted and most responsible vocation—namely, to open the way for the redemption of the world and to prepare for it by the introduction, education, and guidance of the youth of the God-Man. In this work, Saint Joseph cooperated as the instrument of the Holy Spirit. The latter was the guide; Saint Joseph obeyed and carried out the enterprises. It is attractive, instructive, and edifying to consider how the saint corresponded to the guidance of the Holy Spirit. We find in this connection two classes of circumstances in the life of the saint in which his conduct may be a model for us.

Under the first set of circumstances God desires something of us and leaves to us the choice, not revealing His purpose clearly to us, but remaining silent. Saint Joseph probably found himself placed in such circumstances in regard to his espousals with Mary, and afterward in his perplexity as to whether he could take Mary as his wife, and again, on the return from Egypt, when he hesitated about choosing Bethlehem or Nazareth as the domicile of the Holy Family. In such a case, the only thing to be done is to seek advice from a fellow man, or to consult one's own prudence and conscientiousness, or finally, from the circumstances themselves, to discern God's will. Thus may the saint have determined to espouse Mary through the advice obtained from the priests and heads of families. In the torturing perplexity regarding the virginity of his spouse, he consulted his conscience and his good and noble human heart without any regard to the voice of passion, until God Himself manifested His will through an angel. Finally, in his choice of Nazareth as the permanent dwelling place of the Holy Family, he was guided by his own prudence, which judged Archelaus to be as unreliable as Herod, his father. And in this decision the saint was afterward confirmed by God Himself.

In the second set of circumstances, God, indeed, makes known His will and points out the goal but leaves to us the choice and application of the means to reach it. The only thing for one to do in this case is to put aside all attachment to one's own will by conquering oneself, and without fear or hesitation to embrace and carry out God's will with full confidence. Such was Saint Joseph's position when God commanded him to take the Child and fly into Egypt. The purpose was clear, but the means to carry it out were left to Joseph's ingenuity. And he did carry out the command with determination, courage, and perseverance. How unselfish and adaptable must have been the man whom the bare intimation of God's will took from one part of the world to the other, as docile as a lamb, which allows itself to be led with a cord! Shall not Joseph in his obedience be likened to the swift cloud upon which the Lord desires to appear in Egypt (Isa. 19:1)?

Saint Joseph, then, seems to have been raised by God to be a patron in moments when a difficult choice is to be made, especially in the choice of one's vocation in life, a matter of paramount importance to all. If at times a single choice may be fraught with important and serious consequences, how much more the decision that settles one's career for life, as in the case of a vocation or choice of a state of life? In this matter we must follow the example of Saint Joseph and trust in his help. Let us make a few reflections here on how to come to a proper decision in our choice.

First of all, in the question of selecting a proper course of action, this chief and decisive fundamental principle must be followed: in every choice, above all in the choice of a vocation, we must purpose and will nothing but to seek and carry out God's will in regard to our eternal salvation and must not be led by our own will and likes or dislikes unless they agree with God's holy will. To seek or to wish for anything else is wrong and is nothing less than to subject God's will to ours, instead of our will to His; it is to make of the end a means, and of the means an end.

We do not wish to go to God, but we expect God to come to us. The whole task in the matter of election is, therefore, to seek to know God's will in our regard. He is the Lord of our life. He may do what He pleases with it; we may not do so. It belongs to Him, not to us, to determine the ways and means of our service. Man does not create his vocation, but God gives it to him.

In the second place, it follows as a consequence that we are to investigate what may or may not be the matter of our election. Evidently, nothing contrary to God, or sinful, may be the object of our choice. Such a condition is never God's will and can never lead us to our end. The object of our choice must be something morally good, nothing in itself morally wrong; or something that, although indifferent in itself, may under circumstances become good; something, finally, that is consonant with the Church's usage and allowed by her. Hence, the matter of election need not be something already aiming at perfection, such as the priesthood and religious state. God has His designs for each person, and these can lead to their proper goal if no element of moral evil enters in. Hence, God has arranged various states of life in the Church, and in each, with God's help, we may arrive at perfection since perfection essentially consists in the love of God above all things; and this means that we must be and do that which God wishes. Saint Joseph gives proof of this by his example. He was to be, according to God's designs, the model of perfection even in the married state.

This much being supposed, a third consideration regards the manner and means by which we may seek and recognize God's will as regards the state of life or the manner and way in which we are to serve Him and thus save our souls. There are various ways of obtaining a moral assurance as to what God desires. God Himself may make known His good pleasure, as He often did to the saints and as he did on occasion to Saint Joseph when he manifested His will through an angel. In other circumstances, we may obtain light from the interior movements and inspirations of God during prayer, or else from our habitual, natural inclinations and certain suitable qualities that have been bestowed by God for a particular state of life. Finally, sincere and earnest reflection, and the weighing of the advantages and disadvantages regarding one's salvation that occur in various states of life, may help one to a proper decision. What appears best and most advantageous to us, after reasonably considering every side without allowing any mere natural inclination to influence us, may be looked upon as God's will and our vocation. Accordingly, we make a definite decision; and thus, the business of our choice is concluded and the blessing of God will not be wanting. Fervent prayer to God, consultation with spiritual and prudent men, the simple consideration of what advice we would give to a friend for his best interests, and what we ourselves would wish to have done when we come to die, may also serve as indications and be of great advantage to us.

Let us go then to our holy, fatherly friend and adviser, Saint Joseph, when worry besets us in making a proper choice. With much more reason and justice may the words of the Old Testament that Pharaoh spoke concerning Joseph of Egypt, be applied to our saint! "Can we find such another man, that is full of the spirit of God, or a wise man like to him?" (Gen. 41:38). Not less is Saint Joseph's share in the supernatural communications of God than was that of the ancient savior of the people of Egypt. He needs no magic cup or mirrored surface to discover the will of Heaven or the future (Gen. 44:5). He reigns now with his Son and sees reflected in the mirror of God's wisdom the divine will and what is of benefit to our souls. Let us remind him of the worries his own choice of a vocation cost him, and of the interior sorrow of soul during three days of torture caused by his twelve-year-old Son.

It was really the affair of a vocation that dealt this painful blow to his soul, the revelation and preparation of the vocation of the God-Man, the Son of his heart. This distressing episode points to the painful share parents often have in the vocation of their children. Saint Joseph knows from experience both the sorrow and joys connected with the development of a vocation. A rather common opinion in this regard is that those who have chosen according to God's will to lead a wedded life cannot do better than recommend themselves to Joseph for the happy choice of a worthy helpmate. How enviable the happiness of Joseph in his choice of Mary! "A good wife is a good portion" (Sir. 26:3); "A holy and shamefaced woman is grace upon grace" (Sir. 26:19).

Chapter 14

☞

The Model of the Hidden and Interior Life

As we have already remarked, Saint Joseph is called the most obscure among the saints. There is good reason for this remark. His exterior life passes along in obscurity, and his interior life, in which the saint is great and unique, is essentially darkness and shadow.

The exterior view of Saint Joseph's life presents nothing extraordinary or striking. Nothing has come down to us of the early part of his life. A distinct outline of him is obtained only with the coming of Jesus. He is a descendant of the distinguished family of David, but it has no longer any prestige. The greatest part of the saint's life is passed in the little hill town of Nazareth, of very meager importance, not even mentioned in the Old Testament, and in regard to which people shrugged their shoulders as to whether anything worthwhile could originate there (John 1:46). Here, too, the saint does not seem to have held a public office. He was merely known as the carpenter, an occupation in which fame had never before come to anyone. His particular and personal vocation to be the foster father of the Messiah, exalted and sublime in itself and without compare, was the very reason that demanded the profoundest obscurity. The prophets, the Apostles, and the martyrs proclaimed the divinity of Jesus and were rewarded with distinction and glory. Saint Joseph's vocation, as long as he lived, was to hide this divinity. As we have seen, he was the shadow of the heavenly Father, not only in the sense that he was the visible representative of the eternal Father in regard to Jesus, but because under the guise of a natural fatherhood he concealed the divinity of the Son. According to his vocation, then, Saint Joseph is essentially a shadow, which, like an ordinary shadow, passing noiselessly over the earth and covering everything it meets, conceals his Son, Jesus, and even the marvels of his spouse, Mary, her virginity and divine motherhood. The saint throws himself heart and soul into this unique vocation of placing the mantle of obscurity over everything and during his whole life does not deny this vocation, even by a single word. He wishes to be hidden and to remain so. With what revelations could he not have startled the world concerning his virginal spouse, who was the object of important prophecies of old, and the hope of his people?

He sheltered the ardently longed-for Messiah in his tent and yet did not mention a single word about His presence there. The revelations that from time to time light up the infancy of Christ and His person do not come from Joseph. He is only the mute, but interior admirer, "his secret to himself" (Isa. 24:16)! He takes his secret to the grave. He had long disappeared from the scene by the time Jesus wrought His wonders and rose from the tomb, and suddenly transformed the terrible Passion into a reign of glory. Even in the development of the Church the saint was obliged to remain a long time in the shadow, until the day of recompense came in the universal recognition of his merits. Such is the wonderful vocation of Saint Joseph, to be a shadow, to cast a shadow over himself and over all about him and over God Himself.

The Model of the Hidden and Interior Life

The exterior life of the saint is altogether unobtrusive and retiring. But this was not sufficient; the hidden life must needs be an interior life also. In this capacity alone does it fit in with Saint Joseph's office. For his vocation was precisely to be the protector and defender of the hidden life of Jesus. This life was essentially an interior life. Hence, no other saint but an interior one and one who cultivated the interior life could be the defense and protection of the Savior's hidden life. The hidden life is the spiritual and nobler part of a human life, and elevates man to a more exalted and sublime position in human existence than a man's exterior allows us to perceive. The hidden and interior life consists in the participation of the soul, that is, of the inner, spiritual faculties of man, in external affairs, but with a higher, supernatural motive that makes it ever aspire unto God. It is the life of a man from God, for God, and in God.

Therefore, to sum up, the inner life consists above all in purity of heart and freedom from whatever can render us spiritually repulsive and displeasing to God; hence the avoidance of all deliberate and voluntary sin with the accompanying care of and attention to our interior life. Further, the inner life consists in the diligent effort to transform our exterior works into virtue, supernatural virtue, and meritorious activity in God's sight by means of a supernatural motive and good intention. Finally, it consists in the practice of the most intimate union with God by prayer at definitely appointed times and by docility to God's inspirations. Such is, practically, the interior life, and such, too, must have been Saint Joseph's interior life.

How glorious must have been this interior life for Saint Joseph! Who can grasp or comprehend it? We may come nearer to an appreciation of it by a consideration of his vocation and office and of the graces granted to him by God in appropriate measure.

The Truth About Saint Joseph

If Mary obtained such an abundance and such a treasury of graces from the first moment of her existence on earth so that she might become a worthy Mother of God, then, too, Saint Joseph must have received the corresponding apportionment of grace for his office, which in a way approached that of our Blessed Lady. This fund of grace, however, depended entirely on the development of the saint's interior life; indeed, the more modest and retiring the external activities of Saint Joseph were, the more abundant was the increase of his treasury of interior graces.

Surely the circumstances of the saint's life, such as the continual example of our Savior and of the Mother of God, and his intimate companionship with them, could not have been more propitious for the fostering of the interior life. How great must have been the purity of his thoughts, designs, and aspirations, since, like an angel in the vision of the thrice-holy God, he constantly dwelled and moved in the presence of our Lord! How profound and impressive his recollections in all his exterior actions, since his whole life and all his efforts were an undivided service of God and were dedicated to the promotion of the most exalted designs and counsels of God! How ardent the love that was stored away in his heart! How could it be otherwise, since all that happened round about him, what he saw and heard, was a manifestation of the most marvelous mysteries of God's love, unheard-of sources of grace, and revelations of the divine wisdom and beauty itself! As the moon enters a cloud and transfigures it with its light, so must Saint Joseph, who had sunk his whole being into God, have shone interiorly with the divine effulgence itself.

Saint Joseph, therefore, from the fact that he was completely given to the interior life, is a patron of this life unsurpassed by any other. He was not a light beaming into our eyes, but was rather an all-pervading fragrance which all who come near it perceive without knowing its source. And so the fragrance of his interior virtues, as the model of the interior life, continues to pervade the Church of God. Such was his personal greatness, and such it had to be. What in reality would he have been without this interior life, but an empty, passing shadow, a mere nothing before God and man, like the rich and great ones of earth, of whom Holy Scripture says that on awaking they "found nothing in their hands" (Ps. 75:6). Saint Joseph was rich before God in his hidden life.

Such is truly the manner of God's greatness itself. God is hidden, silent, interior, and invisible to us just because He is God and is therefore infinitely happy in and through Himself. We participate in this greatness of God by entering into the interior life, which is essentially a life for God and in God. In this life dwells purity of heart because of intimate converse with God, the mirror of purity; in this life are true riches, because what we do is done for God and becomes pure gold for eternity. In this life, strength of soul abounds because grace, which springs from this union with God, is able to conquer the dangers and difficulties of the exterior life. Let us enter upon the way of the interior life under the guidance of Saint Joseph, by practicing it faithfully, by a calm attention to our interior advancement, by a persevering renewal of a good intention in all our actions, by the practice of prayer and docility to the interior inspirations of God. Without the practice of the interior life, the most hidden life would remain a merely external existence without value and meaning for God and eternity. There is no better guide to the promised land of the interior life than Saint Joseph. To be a citizen of and a great man in this kingdom is the particular property of our saint's holiness and the rich reward he merited by his services during the infancy of Jesus.

Chapter 15

The Model of the Active Life

Man's life is neither a purely exterior life nor a purely interior one. Man is composed of body and soul and, by reason of this dual aspect of his being, has a corresponding activity in his interior as well as in his exterior life. Moreover, man does not in general lead his life in solitude, but in the company of his fellow men and in mutual dealings with them. Hence, his is a mixed life, both interior and exterior.

Thus, too, did Saint Joseph in various ways devote his energies to outward action as well as to the interior life. He was not a hermit, not even one of the Essenes, of whom there were many in the Holy Land. On the contrary, he lived in continual interaction with men; above all with the members of the Holy Family, of which he was the head, support, and protection; with his fellow townsmen also, among whom he dwelt and plied his trade. This necessarily brought him into contact with many people. Saint Joseph, too, made frequent journeys, going several times every year at least to Jerusalem for the chief festivals. The flight from Herod, undertaken at God's command, took him away from his own country as far as Egypt, where he was obliged to sojourn for some time. In this connection the pilgrim's staff, with which ancient art represents the saint, has its appropriate signification. Finally, Saint Joseph was a laboring man, not only in mental and interior work, but in the ordinary exterior, material toil of his hands, by which he had to earn his own living and support the Holy Family. This circumstance is usually represented by the artists of old by means of an axe and an adze, even at the manger of Christ; they are symbols of Joseph's occupation as a carpenter.

For various reasons the external life of Saint Joseph was a well-ordered and perfect life—first, because of the motives that led him to engage in external works. They were the duty of his calling and God's will, which he was not at liberty to resist; again, he was inspired by his love for his family, for Jesus and Mary, and frequently by love for his fellow men and by his noble desire to be of service to them and assist them. Never did the monotony of the work of his vocation, or disgust for it, or tepidity and depression of spirit and heart, or—passing over the quest for pleasures—curiosity and sensible consolation drive him to seek the company of men and the world. Surely the journeys to Bethlehem for the enrollment and through the desert to Egypt, were far from being pleasure trips.

According to the fundamental principles of perfection and sanctity, exterior activity should come forth from the abundance of the interior spirit; it is supposed to be the overflow of one's love for God and for men. It expects man in his external works to give rather than to receive.

Secondly, Saint Joseph's active life was well-ordered and perfect according to the manner and means of his leading it. He was not so preoccupied with external affairs that the care of his interior or his watch over his conscience or his union with God suffered any injury. His exterior activity not only sprang from his interior spirit, but his interior life accompanied, ennobled, and elevated the active by his thought of God and his love of God. In this way his external life amassed a whole treasury of the sublimest virtues. Thus, his exterior life in no wise interfered with his interior. On the contrary, his inner life enriched itself by means of the difficulties, inconveniences, and sufferings that accompanied the external occupation; it enriched itself through the innumerable degrees of merit gained, through the increase of his love for God and through the consolation of having made his fellow men happy.

This is indeed an important lesson that Saint Joseph teaches us here. We are all bound to lead the active life; to lead it properly, we must all labor, and labor in a correct manner. And here we must avoid two mistakes. Sometimes we labor too little. The mistake in this case consists in idleness, in wasting time, in a lack of earnestness and perseverance in devoting our life, our energies, and our talents to the glory of God and the good of our fellow men. Often, however, the mistake is not in really doing nothing, in the omission of all occupation. There is also a busybody idleness and honorable laziness. It consists in useless occupations, in applying oneself to matters that lie outside one's vocation and state of life and are of genuine usefulness neither to us nor to our neighbor. Such work is really no work at all, but one all-engrossing round of amusement, pastime, play, and sport. It is very much like the labor of a canary, which preens its feathers, flits from branch to branch, does its little share of chirping, eats and drinks, and feels quite satisfied. One long round of visit after visit to this club and that, of entertainment after entertainment, of boring oneself with this monotonous pastime and that—and then to expect a deserved rest: Is that work? All this is not work; it is hardly more than doing nothing at all.

The Truth About Saint Joseph

Work in its proper sense is only that which is prescribed, useful, and corresponding to one's calling in life. All else is merely an empty effort to escape ennui and killing monotony. Such activity, however, cannot stand before either God or reason. We must reflect earnestly, in the presence of God and of our conscience, how we spend our time, our lives; how we use our energies and talents, whether in truth something that can stand muster before God is accomplished by our manner of life. He will one day demand of us an account, not only of the abuse of time, but also of its nonuse.

For anyone who respects his dignity as man, it is a shameful thing to eat his daily bread without having earned it, to take it easy and spend his time in uninterrupted recreation, while round about us numberless persons must toil at grinding and galling tasks, and while Christ, too, and His Blessed Mother and His foster father had to procure their sustenance by hard labor. Bread that is not earned is considered stolen bread, at least according to the inspired Word of God: "He that will not work, let him not eat" (2 Thess. 3:10).

We should furthermore examine whether, after fulfilling our own obligatory tasks, something may not be done for the benefit and assistance of our neighbor, for the solution of great problems, and for the relief of the urgent needs of the time by our participating in good works and cooperating with others in charitable enterprises. Does not the commandment of the love of God and of our neighbor exert its binding force perpetually? If we all did our part to labor for the benefit of mankind, the needs of our times would soon find a solution. We may all contribute a considerable share if we only wish to do so. Let us at least do what we can. He who does what he is able to do, does enough.

There is another danger, however: that of doing too much. We labor too much when we engage in external occupations at the expense of our interior spirit, at the expense of our conscience and the things of God; when we are so engrossed in external activities that the more elevated, supernatural motive and intention are neglected; when we do our work without placing our confidence in God; when we wear ourselves out like slaves and beasts of burden, and meanwhile lose every idea and trace of higher and eternal values. Work understood and done in the true and Christian sense, for God and our soul's salvation, is man's duty and honor, the necessary condition of his proper development and happiness for time and eternity. Our portion of Heaven will be precisely what we have acquired for Heaven by our labor here on earth. Understood in any other way, work is a luxury, a detriment, a perversion of all reasonable and Christian intelligence; it is, as our present age amply testifies, a cruel idol, a real Moloch, which seizes a man, body and soul, in its fiery clutches and devours him. Work, in the last analysis, is destined for man, and man is destined for God. Work is not itself the end, but only a means thereto. In order that we may not be demoralized by our external works, we should set aside a definite time during the day for prayer and recollection, and withdraw awhile from other occupations.

In this regard Saint Joseph is a most appropriate model, especially necessary for the present time, which too often and in manifold ways worships labor as an idol. Our saint, combining wisely and in proper measure the interior and exterior occupations of toil, is a timely example for the laboring classes as well as for apostolic men. To him belongs by peculiar right the grace of bestowing the happy faculty of properly combining the interior and exterior activities of our lives. Devotion to Saint Joseph will procure this grace for us.

Chapter 16

⁀

The Patron of Families

We hardly think of Saint Joseph except in the company of Jesus and Mary. He is ever the familiar head of the Holy Family, in its origin, its guidance, its protection, in his labor for Mary and Jesus, and even in his death in their arms. The Holy Family was the scene of his life's work, of his activities, and of his death. This is the ordinary course of man's existence. He moves, lives, and acts in the company of others. Community life is the perfection of human existence. Just as God creates each man according to His own image, so He desires the community life of men to be a reflection of the intimate union of the Blessed Trinity. The Blessed Trinity, in Its unity of nature and plurality of Persons, in Its identity of power and difference of origins, is the most sublime and exalted type of the many societies and organizations that by their development from one another present a picture at once of manifold variety and interior unity. Thus, the entire human race forms a group of the most varying social organizations in both the natural and supernatural orders. Whenever subjects unite under a common head, a society is formed. As a community results from a combination of families, and a state from communities, so, in the supernatural order, the Church results from various religious societies. Saint Joseph, by a particular right, belongs to these various social groups and societies as their patron and heavenly protector.

The first society in order of eminence is the family. The successful existence and continuation of the family depends above all things on authority, which is the foundation of society and preserves it in order; then comes a devoted service of God, which places the family in proper relationship with Him and assures it His blessing; furthermore, labor is necessary for the natural stability and support of the family; finally, there is love, which brings with it domestic peace and happiness. We have already met Saint Joseph in all these situations. Essentially his vocation was to be the head and guide of the Holy Family. He established it by his espousals with Mary. How venerable and amiable his authority appears as representative of the heavenly Father, whose image he is in purity, in wisdom, and in fidelity!

And just as he is the model of piety, so, too, does he give us by his zeal, his earnestness and devout recognition of God's providence, and finally, by his love, the example of labor according to God's pleasure. How peacefully and happily the Holy Family rested under the care of his fatherly regime, even in the midst of trials and contradictions, which are the lot of every family circle on earth and from which not even the Holy Family was exempt. Saint Joseph was the protector, counselor, and consolation of the Holy Family in all these contingencies. And thus in his benign fatherliness he is a born patron and protector of families. His place is deservedly at every domestic hearth, and his image should also be found near that of the heavenly Father and of the Holy Trinity. What family ever existed that was such a perfect image of the Blessed Trinity? Hence, it is most appropriately called the earthly trinity.

The family develops into a community, formed by the collection of many families under a guiding head for the furthering of their temporal welfare; its final development is the state. The Christian state, considered in itself, is a great and sublime idea of God for the welfare of mankind, for the protection of the family, and for the fulfillment of the divine plans in the vast government of the world.

A manifestation of God's gracious designs through the government of a state is seen in the case of Egypt, which under the regime of Saint Joseph's prototype became an instrument of salvation, development, and strength for God's Chosen People, and eventually, for the world's salvation. Saint Joseph, it is true, never held the reins of a secular government; and yet, he was in a much more significant sense "the father of the king" (see Gen. 45:8), of the greatest king, of the King of kings. At any rate the government of the Holy Family demanded more virtue and sanctity than did the rule of Pharaoh's kingdom. Saint Joseph saved not only one country and one people from starvation, but furnished the Bread of Eternal Life to the whole human race. He is a shining example for every ruler of a kingdom or head of a community by his virtues, which befit such an office — namely, wisdom, a kindly, provident foresight, and a divine and heavenly statesmanship; and he is no less a model for subjects by his obedience and his submission to secular authority. He alone governs well who knows how to obey. This was the reason why great kingdoms and mighty dynasties of old selected Saint Joseph as the protector of their families and countries. Nor has the saint failed to protect them in time of need. But other times have come; new stars have risen in the firmament of statecraft; new methods have attracted political rulers. "Now they know not Joseph" (see Exod. 1:8) has become true of our saint. But has the lot of princes and people changed for the better? Who will dare to assert this?

In the third place, the Church, the vast supernatural society of men and the family of God on earth, demands our attention. As in the case of every society, so as regards the Church, the real question is its government. This is represented in the organized, hierarchical priesthood, which establishes, supports, and perpetuates the whole Church. Now, the priestly authority consists above all in its power over the true Body of Christ, really and substantially present in the Blessed Sacrament of the Altar and forever continuing its life in the Church. From this power, too, emanates authority over the Mystical Body of Christ, which the faithful of the Church constitute; the power, namely, to teach them, to govern them, to reconcile them with God, to bless them, and to pray for them.

The Holy Family was the type and starting point of the Church. Saint Joseph was the regularly constituted head of this family, its father, protector, guide, and support and, for that very reason, belongs in a particular way to the Church, which was the objective purpose of the Holy Family's existence, and in a way, its spiritual extension and perpetuation. The more important members of the Church are the priests; and thus Saint Joseph has a special relationship to the order of priesthood, and this in a twofold manner. First, as regards their office and priestly functions. As we have seen, Saint Joseph possessed a wonderful power over our Savior Himself. To some extent he was the means of bringing the Redeemer to us; for he reared Him, nurtured Him, protected and sheltered Him. His office and vocation were especially concerned with the person of Christ; his entire activity centered about the Savior. Saint Joseph's life and office, then, were of a priestly nature, even as the priestly functions are primarily connected with the Blessed Sacrament. The saint gave us the Savior, not indeed, directly, as the priest gives Him to us by means of the words of consecration, although he did so by a more direct and far more important service than that of all the other ministers at the altar. The second relation of Saint Joseph to the priesthood consists in his virtues, which are again correspondingly priestly—namely, the spirit of faith, purity of heart, humility, and zeal for souls. We have had occasion to witness the saint's life in these various particulars. There cannot be a more beautiful and personal model for priests than Saint Joseph.

There exists in the Church of God another kind of family, especially near and dear to our saint and belonging to him—namely, the religious orders, or the collection of different institutes of the religious life. In general the religious life is a school of perfection, because it is the duty of one's vocation therein to aim at perfection. Perfection consists essentially in the love of God, which indeed is the case in every state of life. Religious perfection differs from that of the secular state in the means used to aim at perfection and to reach it. Whereas the secular state uses only the means that are essentially necessary for the acquisition and practice of love, namely, the observance of the Commandments of God, the religious state employs means of supererogation—namely, the observance of the evangelical counsels, the vows of poverty, chastity, and obedience, which in themselves are not obligatory for anyone, but are yet the best means to perfection since they remove in a particularly efficacious way the impediments to the love of God. These are: attachment to worldly goods, which is removed by poverty; inclination to sensual pleasures, which is opposed by chastity; and undue attachment to one's will and independence, which is subdued by obedience. Besides these general means, common to all orders and essentially constituting the religious state, each individual order has its own particular means to arrive at the perfection of love, whether in a contemplative or active life, according as it especially devotes itself to its own perfection or the salvation of souls. Hence, the orders are divided into active and contemplative orders.

All these considerations are so many reasons for establishing a very close relationship of the religious orders to Saint Joseph, and give them a special right to his help and protection. What else was our saint's main purpose in life than perfection in the love of God? Did he not actually lead a life of poverty, chastity, and obedience? And to what perfection of love did he not attain? He combined the contemplative with the active life in a most perfect manner. Truly he is the distinctively appropriate model for the varying types of perfection that have their existence and find expression in the different religious institutes. Who has come closer than Joseph to our divine Savior and Lord, the most sublime model of the union of both states of life? That is why Saint Joseph is quite at home in all the religious orders, and by their very vocation, as it were, belongs to them all, the contemplative, active, and mixed orders. Hence, by degrees every order acknowledged him as its special protector. Moreover, those other families, the foreign missions, are dedicated to him in a special manner. Where did the Magi, the firstfruits of the pagan world, find the Savior but in the company of Joseph? He it was who first carried the Savior into a pagan country. All these facts are reason enough for the saint's particular predilection for these distant families of God's Church—the foreign missions.

Thus, there is not a single important organization or society of the Church in which the saint by every right is not welcome and made to feel at home and to be, as we say, one of the family. All the variety of experience common to family life on earth are for us, as well as for him, cherished and sacred remembrances of the life, sufferings, and joys that were his particular portion on earth in his relation to his divine Son and his beloved spouse, Mary. Saint Joseph sanctified himself as head of the Holy Family and thus by his beautiful example sanctified family life. In the domain of family life God has, therefore, constituted him a heavenly patron. It is a beautiful and a rich world created by God, this varied family life on earth. It is dear then to Saint Joseph as the work of God and is of paramount importance for the honor of God and the well-being of man. Especially is Saint Joseph's help needed in our day when God's enemy has directed his attack precisely against the family in order to desecrate and destroy it, thereby converting it into an instrument of malediction and making of it an earthly hell. In the face of these evils Saint Joseph, as patron of the family, must intervene; and as of old he arose to save the child and His mother, so today he must arise to safeguard the sanctity of the home.

We shall conclude this chapter with a reflection that explains the reason for another title often, and rightfully, given to Saint Joseph. Since he is naturally the patron of all societies and organizations in the Church, Pope Pius IX made him patron of the Universal Church. And thus the glorious title of patriarch also falls by right to his share. The patriarchs were the tribal heads of the families of the one-time Chosen People, and theirs was the honor and special privilege to prepare for the Savior's Incarnation. Our saint also belongs to this line of patriarchs, for he was one of the last descendants of the family of David and one of the nearest forebears of Christ according to the flesh; in fact, as husband of Mary, the Mother of God, and as the foster father of the Savior, he was directly connected with Christ. He is, therefore, the culmination of the Old Testament and hence, too, the beginning of the New, which, as Pope Leo XIII says, took its rise with the establishment of the Holy Family.[8] Saint Joseph then, as patriarch, belongs both to the Old and to the New Testament. He is consequently the patriarch of patriarchs, in the noblest sense the chief of all, since the New Testament infinitely surpasses the Old in every respect — in extent of territory and in the number of its progeny as well as in dignity. Saint Joseph is in truth the most venerable, exalted, and supremely amiable of all the patriarchs. He places one hand in blessing on the Old Covenant and the other on the New; he is the princely dispenser of benedictions to the one and the other. Who is like Joseph?

[8] Leo XIII, Encyclical *Quamquam Pluries* (On Devotion to Saint Joseph), August 15, 1889.

Chapter 17

⌒

The Patron of the Afflicted

Everything in the world is fraught with sorrow, and no mortal here below can escape suffering. It clings to human nature and dogs its footsteps. Indeed the whole history of the human race is but one great tragedy of a thousand difficulties and contradictions. Suffering began with the fall of our first parents and ends only with death. All this must be quite reasonable, for a wise and merciful God has so ordained it. Through suffering we were redeemed, and only through suffering do we share in the Redemption. Many are the souls that will be taught and saved only by suffering. And so the Cross is the portion of all men, even of the saints, and hence, of Saint Joseph also.

Indeed, his share of suffering was exceedingly great because of his close relationship to the divine Savior. All the mysteries of our Lord's life are more or less mysteries of suffering. Even Bethlehem and Nazareth have their Cross. Wherever the Savior pillowed His head, traces of the crown of thorns were to be found. How long the divine Child dwelled with Joseph, and how often He rested in his arms and on his breast! Surely the cross could not be wanting to the saint. The cross of labor followed him everywhere; poverty pressed upon him, less on his own account than on that of his divine Son and his holy spouse, Mary, whom he saw so poorly and unbecomingly provided for in this world. Even the lack of necessary shelter afflicted him more than once. Hard-hearted people refused to open the door to him; blood-thirsty persecutors and men full of deadly hate, sought both his life and that of his child.

Nor was he spared even domestic crosses, owing to misunder-standings in regard to the holiest and most cherished of beings, Jesus and Mary, who were all to him. Again and again they were the occasion of bitter crosses to him. Keen indeed must have been the suffering caused by the uncertainty regarding Mary's virginity, by the circumcision of Jesus and the bestowal of His name, which pointed to future misfortunes. Profoundly pain-ful, too, must have been the prophecy of Simeon, the flight into Egypt, and the disappearance of Jesus at the Paschal feast, which occurrence itself strikingly foreshadowed the Passion. These mysteries were like a bloody summit of Calvary in the life of Saint Joseph.

To these sufferings was surely added that interior, gnawing sorrow of the saint at the sight of the sins of his people and of the calamities that threatened them. Truly, suffering and contradic-tion as well as blessings were the lot of the Joseph of the New Testament. If his afflictions are not great and extraordinary when compared with the terrible sufferings experienced by the Mother of God at the foot of the Cross, they nevertheless wounded his heart most bitterly because these sufferings had as their object and source his highest good, his divine Son, and because his love for Him was inexpressibly great.

The sufferings of Saint Joseph are therefore noble, admirable, and sublime on account of their cause, which was none other than the sufferings of the Savior Himself, and on account of the manner in which he bore and endured these contradictions. The greatest triumph of art, it is said, is to represent suffering in a sublime and attractive manner. But it is infinitely more difficult to bear suffering properly and in a Christian manner. Here the saint gives us a splendid example. No sound of complaint or impatience escapes him; in general, he must have been a man of silence, since Holy Writ has not handed down to us a single word of his. He submitted to all in the spirit of faith, humility, confidence, and infinite love, and cheerfully bore all in union with the Savior and His Mother, glad to be able to suffer something with them and for them.

God, in His turn, never forsook the saint in his trials. Everywhere God was with him, and everything went well. The trials, too, vanished and were converted at last into consolation and joy. After the misunderstanding concerning Mary came the message of the angel, which made Joseph the happiest of men. After the rebuff at Bethlehem came the joy and happiness of the birth of Christ and the adoration of shepherds and kings. The trial of the flight into Egypt was rewarded by the joyful return to Galilee; the cruel loss of the Child and the three days of heartrending search for Him were amply repaid by the happy finding of Him in the Temple and the blissful years of the hidden life.

It seems that God purposely so constituted and intended the life of Saint Joseph to keep very vividly before our eyes the truth that our life on earth is but a succession of good and bad days, and that we must make up our minds to accept both and to preserve toward them a proper attitude of soul. After all, the days of peace and joy ordinarily predominate, just as oil floats upon the water. We must not forget this and must gratefully accept whatever God sends us. We must courageously carry the burdens of the harder days in thanksgiving for the joyful ones and, during the time of consolation, must prepare for suffering.

To use both joy and sorrow in the proper manner is a great art. The cross tries to cast us down through impatience, distrust, and despair, while joy and gladness, on the other hand, would undo us by means of self-elation, frivolity, and the awful danger of forgetfulness of God. Like Saint Joseph, let us ever remain the same in time of suffering and of joy. The fact that we rejoice in happy circumstances, while we keenly feel the bitterness of the cross, is not counted against us by our benign Maker. Such is our nature. Let us bear all in the spirit of faith, of confidence, and of a grateful attitude toward God. In a happy eternity we shall not thank God for anything as much and as fervently as for the sufferings that He deigned to send us during our sojourn on earth and that, after the example of Saint Joseph, we endured with patience and heartfelt love for Jesus and Mary.

Chapter 18

The Patron of a Happy Death

We have seen that man's necessities and sufferings on earth are many and manifold. One such trial is the lot of all. We all belong to the confraternity of death, just as we all are subject to sin. Death is the sad penalty of sin; no one escapes it.

Death is a hard and bitter lot for our poor nature. Above all it is the end of our corporal, physical life. The intimate union of soul and body that conditions and constitutes our earthly life is dissolved by death. The separation is violent and painful because the body, through weakness and dissolution, abandons the soul and forces it to leave its crumbling dwelling place. The separation is furthermore a humiliating one because it is a punishment of sin, a sort of execution that separates body and soul, the two guilty associates in sin. The soul is handed over to eternity, the body to the earth, where by degrees it crumbles to dust and becomes something without a name. Death, then, is a bitter trial, a profound humiliation, the most stubborn of struggles, and the keenest of sufferings.

Death, moreover, is not only the end of our earthly life but also the beginning of the life beyond, the entrance into eternity and the commencement of our everlasting, unchangeable destiny, of the nature, greatness, and immensity of which, as regards punishments as well as rewards, we have no adequate concept. Death, finally, is the occasion of our meeting with God, before whom we must appear to be judged, punished or rewarded, justly, strictly, irrevocably, for all eternity.

In a word, to die is a lonely, helpless, and joyless thing. No one of our loved ones can help us. No human hand can penetrate into the inner sanctuary where the last, desperate struggle is being waged. We are alone, all alone. Only Heaven can come to our assistance.

At such an hour it is truly an important matter to have a kind patron who will aid and console us, and who can furnish us the means to die a good, edifying, peaceful, and holy death. Hardly a better patron than Saint Joseph could be found, for what deathbed was ever as beautiful as his must have been? All the conditions necessary to render his departure from earth a most happy and consoling one were united there. The past showed the saint a life of innocence and purity; a life of the most genuine and sublime virtue; a life of untold merit in the service of Jesus, of Mary, of the Church, and of the whole of mankind; a life of labor, fatigue, and suffering, borne in the spirit of patience, of faith, and with the noblest love. This retrospect gave him no cause for regret or fear, but all was full of hope. We learn from his life what his death was. Does not everything combine to render his death not only good, but consoling and even joyful? He died in the arms of Jesus, his Son and God, and in the arms of Mary; both, especially at that moment, compensated all his endeavors for them with unheard of graces. They were helpers and consolers who not only supported his frail body, but who with powerful, soothing graces refreshed and rejoiced the heart and soul of the dying saint, while the Holy Spirit replenished him with a Heaven of consolation and joy.

The glimpse into the future reveals to our saint his happy meeting with his gloriously risen Son after a short stay in the quiet abode of Limbo, where the saintly souls of the Old Testament awaited their transfiguration; he sees the kingdom of eternal joy, where the Heavenly Father receives his worthy representative and faithful administrator, ministers to him, and sets him over all His treasures (Luke 12:37). There was something extraordinarily grand and majestic in his departure from life, like the quiet effulgence of the setting sun, which at the end of a day's work gazes back with rapturous joy on all it has accomplished and quietly sinks to rest in the bosom of God. There exists no more precious masterpiece of grace, no incense more fragrant before the Lord, than the death of a saint (Ps. 115:15).

Saint Joseph's death is also a touching and desirable example for us. He can help us to make our death similarly beautiful, and that in a threefold way. First, the example of his passing encourages us not to fear a death in Christ and with Christ, full of faith, hope, and love of Him. The holy protecting powers that hovered near the saint's deathbed and consoled him are at our command also in the means of grace given us by Mother Church, among these being Christ Himself in holy Viaticum. It was in the shadow of death that Christ had His Cross erected, and now He Himself comes to assist us mightily in our last struggle. With Him and in Him we are to make the last, hard sacrifices. He accepts them mercifully and unites them to His.

Secondly, Saint Joseph helps us to prepare for a good and consoling death by the example of his holy life, which teaches us the proper preparation for dying happily. The last act of our lives must be prepared just as carefully as any other work. Nothing is more certain than death and nothing more important, since at that moment our eternity is decided. Hence it must be prepared for in life and by means of our lives. Death is not merely the end of life, but the echo of life. Indeed we should not only prepare for death, but should be always in a state of preparation; for death comes soon, quickly, and unexpectedly, and only once. The beautiful life of our saint, his freedom from sin; his pious, devout life; his constant, meritorious self-denial, filled with love for Jesus and Mary, teaches us in what this preparation consists.

Thirdly, Saint Joseph obtains for us a happy, trustful, consoling death by our devotion to him. These pious practices in his honor are so many compacts formed, indeed, in life, but having their efficacious reward and blessing at the hour of death.

Hence, it is well for us frequently to recommend our last hour to Saint Joseph. He will not be wanting in his clients on that important occasion. How happy we shall be to have Saint Joseph close our eyes in death (see Gen. 46:4)!

Chapter 19

☙

Joseph Is a "Growing Son"

Saint Joseph, as we have seen, is inseparably bound to the person and life of our divine Savior and is thus built into the foundations of Christendom. For this very reason, proper recognition of him and veneration for him could not be lacking in the Church. What the Gospel, the historical source of knowledge of our Faith, establishes concerning our saint, is, as it were, the germ and the root from which the tree of manifold devotion to him sprang forth and kept developing more and more. But the truth about the grain of mustard seed and its hardly noticeable, silent, slow growth is the law of Christianity, which must be fulfilled in the case of every Christian, even in our Lord's regard, and hence in that of His foster father also — in fact, very particularly so. Slowly but steadily did devotion to Saint Joseph increase. We may compare its growth to the course of the natural year, and distinguish and recognize early spring, spring itself, and the bright summer day in the veneration paid to Saint Joseph.

Early spring as regards the devotion to Saint Joseph lasted a long time, a very long time, even up to the twelfth century. Whereas our Lord, His Blessed Mother, and many martyrs were the object of public veneration and religious festivals, relatively few vestiges of external devotion to Joseph can be found in the first centuries. Probably this circumstance is attributed to the fact that in the earlier history of the Church, the memory of the martyrs was celebrated rather than that of the other saints. The great task of the Church at the commencement of Christianity was to defend and prove the divinity of Christ and His supernatural, virginal birth against the attacks of the pagans and heretics, rather than to emphasize and throw light upon His human origin and earthly relationships. For this reason, the public veneration of our saint was forced into the background. This seems to be a stroke of Divine Providence, which appoints to each creature its peculiar work and permanently adapts the circumstances of life to the task. While Saint Joseph in his earthly career, by means of his foster fatherhood, for a time cast a shadow over the divinity of Christ, on the other hand, by his disappearance and unobtrusiveness he was to serve as the dark background, as it were, for the more effective light illumining Christ's divinity.

Meanwhile, the first centuries are not without their glorious testimonies to Joseph's greatness. The Doctors and Fathers of the Church, and ecclesiastical writers, such as Justin, Origen, Ephrem, Chrysostom, Jerome, and Chrysologus, in their writings and homilies give Saint Joseph his due honor. Later on, two feasts in honor of the saint obtained prominence in the Eastern Church and especially in its monasteries. Christian art, too, as we have seen, gives the saint very honorable recognition in keeping with the importance of his position as the protector and the refuge of the Holy Family; such, particularly, are the mosaics of the fifth century in the Church of Santa Maria Maggiore, Rome. In the Middle Ages the artists seem to neglect him altogether.

Joseph Is a "Growing Son"

The springtme of the devotion to Saint Joseph began, at least in the Western Church, with the twelfth century. At this date, indeed, the veneration paid to the saint is historically verified. Eminent voices, for instance, those of Saint Bernard, Ludolph of Saxony, and Margaret of Cortona, proclaimed his honor, while in the communities of the Dominican and Franciscan orders the devotion was already happily flourishing. The spring in all its fullness first appeared in the fifteenth century, when at the Council of Constance (1414) the learned Gerson enthusiastically requested a general feast for the Church in honor of the saint, while his master, the celebrated Cardinal Peter d'Ailly, gave to the public his work on the prerogatives of Saint Joseph. Feasts in honor of the saint were already celebrated in some places, and soon churches dedicated to him arose in various parts of Europe. This movement was greatly fostered by the sermons of three popular preachers of the Franciscan order: Saint Bernardine of Siena (1418), Bernardine of Feltre (1487), and Bernardine of Busto (1500), as well as by the celebrated book of the Dominican Isidoro Isolani and the theological treatises of the Jesuit Francisco Suárez (d. 1617), and particularly by the efforts of Saint Teresa of Jesus (d. 1582), who placed no less than fifteen of her convents under the protection of Saint Joseph.

The devotion reached its full summer day only in the seventeenth century. The Jesuit Pierre Coton (d. 1626) introduced it into the French court where Jacques-Bénigne Bossuet delivered his renowned panegyric on the saint, which had the effect of inducing Urban VIII to establish the feast of Saint Joseph as a holy day of obligation for France. Emperor Leopold I in thanksgiving for the birth of an heir to the throne—namely, Joseph I, and for the delivery of Vienna from the danger of the Turks, placed all his states under the protection of the saint, and with the permission of the Pope had the feast of the Espousals of Joseph and Mary solemnly celebrated in his dominions. Clement XI (1714) composed the festal office of the saint and prescribed it for the whole Church. Finally, Benedict XIII (1726), at the request of Emperor Charles VI and of a number of religious orders, inserted the name of Saint Joseph in the Litany of All the Saints. This zeal of the fifteenth, sixteenth, seventeenth, and eighteenth centuries for the honor of Saint Joseph was crowned at last in the nineteenth, when Pius IX (1847) realized the desires of the many ardent clients of the saint by extending the feast of the Patronage of Saint Joseph to the whole Church, by consecrating the month of March entirely to him, and by declaring Saint Joseph patron of the Universal Church. This was done in 1870, and thus the whole Kingdom of Christ on earth was placed at the saint's feet. Leo XIII, too, on the fifteenth of August 1889, published a fervent encyclical on the veneration of Saint Joseph.

As far as we can see, nothing can be added to do him further honor. In the Orient, almost from the very beginning of Christianity; in the West, certainly since the twelfth century, faith has implanted the devotion to the saint in the hearts of the Christian people, and this devotion, developing ever more clearly, fully, and joyfully, became better known. This popular devotion to the saint, which had been inspired by the Holy Spirit, was welcomed with joy and accepted by the Church, which blessed and fostered it. Century after century new stones were added to the saint's earthly temple of honor. The faithful and the world of art (especially since the fifteenth century), eminent writers and learned men, the religious orders, great saints and popes have labored to place Saint Joseph on an exalted throne of honor, surpassed in splendor only by that of the Mother of God and his divine foster Son.

Joseph Is a "Growing Son"

Thus, the Lord has fulfilled His word, "that He will honor those who honor Him," that "the Keeper of the Lord will be glorified" (Prov. 27:18), and that He will place "His faithful servant over all His treasures." How splendidly the Lord rewarded on earth the humble services of His foster father and made good and repaired the temporary withholding of his recognition and veneration in the Church. All the faithful assembled at the throne of Joseph cry to him, their protector: "Our salvation is in thy hands, turn thine eyes toward us, and joyfully will we serve the King" (Gen. 47:25).

According to Holy Writ the Egyptian Joseph was the typical "growing son" (Gen. 49:22). Every contradiction served only to open a new avenue to power and promotion; as in the tents of his father, so in the house of the Egyptian priest of the sun, so in the prison dungeon, whose gates open to allow him to ascend to his sovereign position over all Egypt. Our Saint Joseph, however, has infinitely surpassed his glorious prototype. In him the prophecies that the dying patriarch Jacob made to Joseph have their complete fulfillment. "Joseph is a growing son. The Almighty shall bless thee with the blessings of Heaven above and with the blessings of the deep. Thy blessings are mightier than the blessings of the fathers of the Old Covenant; they reach unto the everlasting hills; they are on Joseph's head, upon the crown of one chosen among his brethren" (Gen. 49:22, 25, 26). The promises of God are fulfilled slowly, but most certainly and admirably.

Chapter 20

℘

A Saint for All

It is recorded in Holy Scripture that the people of Israel, in grateful memory of their deliverer and benefactor, took the remains of Joseph with them at their departure from Egypt into the Holy Land, and buried them in the country of Samaria (Exod. 13:19). We, as Christians, must not be less appreciative of our Saint Joseph. We are indebted to him in an infinitely higher degree. Hence, we are to cultivate a heartfelt devotion to Saint Joseph.

The devotion may be practiced in the following way. Fervent clients of the saint do not allow a day to pass without performing some small acts of devotion in his honor, recommending themselves to him and asking his protection. For this purpose, there is a short, very touching chaplet of the Joys and Sorrows of Saint Joseph, enriched with indulgences by Pius VII, Gregory XVI, and Pius IX. Each week, moreover, has a day set aside, Wednesday, which is especially dedicated to him. This practice, which dates from the seventeenth century, originated in the Benedictine Monastery of Chalons in France. In the ecclesiastical year there are two feasts of the saint that are celebrated throughout the whole Church, and one that is restricted to certain localities.

The Truth About Saint Joseph

The two feasts of general observance are the feast of Saint Joseph, celebrated on March 19, which originated in the fifteenth century under Sixtus IV, and the Solemnity of Saint Joseph the Worker, celebrated on May 1. The third festival, the Espousals of Mary and Joseph, celebrated on January 23, was first kept in the sixteenth century in the convents of the Franciscans and the Dominicans; in the time of Emperor Leopold I the feast was extended by Innocent XI to the whole Church, but since the reign of Pius X it is celebrated in only a limited number of places.

Moreover, an entire month, March, has been especially dedicated to the veneration of Saint Joseph by Pius IX and Leo XIII. Besides, each of his feasts may be introduced by a fitting novena.

And so, devotion to Saint Joseph occupies an important position in the order of feasts of the ecclesiastical year, and in this regard all we have to do is simply to follow our holy Mother the Church. Motives for practicing this devotion present themselves in sufficient number in consequence of our daily personal necessities, difficulties, and trials. Let us not forget to fly to the saint for protection and to recommend to him our needs. The clients of the saint are particularly fond of asking three favors of him every day: first, the grace to grow more and more in the intimate love of Jesus and Mary; secondly, the grace to unite properly, as he did, the interior with the exterior life; and finally, the grace of a happy, edifying, and consoling death. His life was especially notable from this threefold viewpoint. Thus, it would appear that the saint had been endowed by God with a special power to procure these graces for us.

In conclusion, we need but gather briefly and cursorily a few motives for practicing devotion to Saint Joseph. First, he deserves our veneration because he is so worthy of it and is so great a saint. How close his relationship to us and how much we owe to him!

As foster father of Jesus he is connected most intimately with the earliest history of our religion. Our Savior acknowledged him as His earthly father; He was subject to him; He wished to be indebted to His legal parent for everything in the temporal order; He sanctified Joseph by His many years of familiar communion with him. No relic has ever been so consecrated by close contact with the Incarnate Word of God as was the saint. His eyes, his hands, his arms received a consecration as often as they looked upon or carried the divine Child. And with what unfathomable love the saint's heart throbbed for his foster son! What Joseph did for Christ, he has done for us, God's people. We must return thanks to the saint for this. We shall never be able to extol or repay his services to us in a worthy manner.

Secondly, Saint Joseph deserves our veneration because he is so amiable a saint. He is the chosen spouse of Mary, her protection and her solace, the protector, angel guardian, and saint of the childhood of Jesus. He makes his appearance with the Child Jesus and with Him vanishes. Hence, the symbol and badge of his vocation and of its purpose are none other than those of the Christ Child Himself, whom he ever carries in his arms and presses to his heart. How amiable a saint he is through his calling, and especially through his virtues, summed up in his fatherliness, his purity, fidelity, constancy, unselfishness, humility, wisdom, and love. All these are such attractive virtues, so inspiring with confidence, that of themselves they invite us to choose him as our counselor, our provider, and our father in all our necessities, even as Mary and Jesus trustfully placed all their concerns in his hands.

In the third place, the saint deserves our trustful affection because he is such a practical and resourceful saint, as though specially fashioned to be our helper in difficulty and trial. He has lived an entire human life with all its vicissitudes, joys, and sufferings. Indeed God seems to have so arranged the circumstances of his life's vocation that, as Pope Leo XIII in his encyclical on the saint so graphically describes, he may well serve as our model and pattern in every circumstance of life, and with his own knowledge and experience come to our assistance. From his own experience he knows how heavy the burden of the father of a family may be in consequence of want, poverty, and persecution; he knows what is meant by superior and inferior; he has in deed and in truth sanctified the state of matrimony and virginity, life in the cloister and in the world, the contemplative and the active life, and has crowned his existence with a most blessed death.

Thus, God has given him the power to lend his aid and protection in all our concerns, and to bring them to a happy and successful issue. It is especially the crosses and perplexities of everyday life that bring his life so close to our lives and cause him to assist us so kindly and sympathetically. He is the great and universal master of the prince's house and the father of God's family. Hence he always knows when to help and has the power and the heart to do so. What was said of Joseph of old, "that God made all he did to prosper in his hand" (Gen. 39:3), holds in far greater measure of our saint. Hence, his name is most lovingly venerated in all lands and conditions of life; and although his clients be without number, they cannot exhaust his power and his love.

Finally, Saint Joseph is not only a practical saint but seems especially fashioned by God for our modern times. He is, we might say, the modern saint. Each period of history has its particular dangers and needs, and God in His infinite wisdom and goodness provides it with corresponding remedies. For several decades a new force has been developing and today is fully developed. It is the power of the sons of untiring labor, but not the well-ordered, God-ordained labor based on trust in God. This latter type of labor gives no cause for anxiety since it has been in the world from the beginning of the human race, is the lot of all men, and is their honor and privilege. God has blessed it and in His Son sanctified and almost deified it. We fear rather that restless drudgery, that toil divorced from God and the supernatural; we fear that unbounded self-seeking, greed for money, possessions, pleasures; we fear the power of a proud and stubborn self-sufficiency and self-deification; we fear the power of a crude, untrammeled self-government that would erect its throne without God and the Church, on the ruins of the old order and existing institutions, yea, upon the ruins of family life itself. The true names of this monster, the unholy progeny of all social disorders, are unbelief, materialism, revolution, anarchy, class and racial hatred.

Where shall we find the help provided by God for these evil times? Where is the new man, the new power prepared by God to take a decided stand on behalf of justice, order, God's glory, and man's welfare? Who can it be but the exalted personage of unselfish attachment to duty, the man of obedience, faith, and trust in God, of humility and willing devotion to labor? Who but Saint Joseph, the calm, earnest man of noble ancestry, but poor and humble by choice, Saint Joseph, who on a former occasion saved the nascent Church, then, represented by the Holy Family, from the bloody hands of a ruthless persecutor? Why else has God been preparing a way in the Church during the last century for the devotion to Saint Joseph? Why else has He exalted him just at these critical times to the position of protector of the universal Church? He is indeed the man in whose hands God has placed the destinies of the Church. Let us then trust in him. We shall certainly not be confounded.

The Truth About Saint Joseph

No words can inspire us with greater confidence in Saint Joseph in all our needs than those of Saint Teresa of Avila,[9] with which we shall conclude:

> I cannot remember having asked Saint Joseph for anything which he did not obtain. I am quite amazed when I consider the great favors our Lord has shown me through the intercession of this blessed saint, and the many dangers, both of soul and body, from which he has delivered me. It seems that to other saints our Lord has given the power to succor us in only one kind of necessity, but this glorious saint, I know by my experience, assists us in all kinds of necessities; hence our Lord, it appears, wishes us to understand that as He was obedient to him when on earth (for he was called His father; and being, as it were, His tutor, he could command Him), so now in heaven He grants him whatever he asks. This truth many others also have experienced, who have recommended themselves to him by my desire; many are now devoted to him, and I myself have fresh experience of his power.... Would that I could persuade all men to be devout to this glorious saint, by reason of the great experience I have had of the blessings he obtains from God! I have never known anyone who was truly devoted to him, who performed particular devotions in his honor, that did not advance more in virtue; for he assists in a special manner those souls that recommend themselves to him. During many years I was accustomed to ask some particular favor of him on his feast day, and I remember it was always granted; ...

---

[9] *Autobiography*, chap. 6.

I only request, for the love of God, that whoever will not believe me, will prove the truth of what I say; for he will see by experience how great a blessing it is to recommend oneself to this glorious patriarch and to be devout to him. I know not how anyone can think of the Queen of Angels, who suffered so much on account of the Child Jesus, and not give thanks to Saint Joseph for the assistance he gave them.

Sophia Institute

Sophia Institute is a nonprofit institution that seeks to nurture the spiritual, moral, and cultural life of souls and to spread the Gospel of Christ in conformity with the authentic teachings of the Roman Catholic Church.

Sophia Institute Press fulfills this mission by offering translations, reprints, and new publications that afford readers a rich source of the enduring wisdom of mankind.

Sophia Institute also operates two popular online Catholic resources: CrisisMagazine.com and CatholicExchange.com.

Crisis Magazine provides insightful cultural analysis that arms readers with the arguments necessary for navigating the ideological and theological minefields of the day. *Catholic Exchange* provides world news from a Catholic perspective as well as daily devotionals and articles that will help you to grow in holiness and live a life consistent with the teachings of the Church.

In 2013, Sophia Institute launched Sophia Institute for Teachers to renew and rebuild Catholic culture through service to Catholic education. With the goal of nurturing the spiritual, moral, and cultural life of souls, and an abiding respect for the role and work of teachers, we strive to provide materials and programs that are at once enlightening to the mind and ennobling to the heart; faithful and complete, as well as useful and practical.

Sophia Institute gratefully recognizes the Solidarity Association for preserving and encouraging the growth of our apostolate over the course of many years. Without their generous and timely support, this book would not be in your hands.

www.SophiaInstitute.com
www.CatholicExchange.com
www.CrisisMagazine.com
www.SophiaInstituteforTeachers.org

Sophia Institute Press® is a registered trademark of Sophia Institute.
Sophia Institute is a tax-exempt institution as defined by the
Internal Revenue Code, Section 501(c)(3). Tax I.D. 22-2548708.